Leib Weihnachtskuchen

and his Child

Karl Emil Franzos

*Leib Weihnachtskuchen
and
his Child*

Translated by Michael Mitchell

ARIADNE PRESS

THE ASCOG PRESS

Translation copyright © Michael Mitchell 2005
First published in 2005 by The Ascog Press
Kirkokerry, Millhouse, Tighnabruaich
Argyll PA21 2BW

Ariadne Press, 270 Goins Court, Riverside
CA 92507, USA

Distributed in the UK by Gazelle Book Services Limited
Hightown, White Cross Mills, South Rd, Lancaster, LA1 4XS

The right of Michael Mitchell to be identified as the translator of the work
has been asserted herein in accordance with the Copyright, Designs and
Patents Act 1988.

All rights reserved. This book is sold subject to the condition that it shall
not, by way of trade or otherwise, be lent, resold, hired out or otherwise
circulated without the publisher's prior consent in any form of binding or
cover other than that in which it is published and without a similar condition
including this condition being imposed on the subsequent purchaser.

All the characters in this book are fictitious and any resemblance to actual
people, living or dead, is purely imaginary.

British Library Cataloguing in Publication Data
A catalogue record for this book is available from the British Library

Library of Congress Cataloging in Publication data available on request
United Kingdom: The Ascog Press: 0-9545989-0-3
USA: Ariadne Press 1-57241-137-6

Typeset by Amolibros, Milverton, Somerset
This book production has been managed by Amolibros
Printed and bound by T J International Ltd, Padstow, Cornwall, UK

Introduction

Karl Emil Franzos (1848-1904), the son of a doctor, a liberal Jew, was born in Czortkow (now Chortkiv) and grew up in Czernowitz (now Chernivsty), both towns, until 1918 part of the Habsburg Empire. He studied law, but did not want to work as an advocate; a position of judge was barred to him, as a Jew, and he refused to convert in order to advance his career. He became a journalist and edited important literary magazines in Vienna and, after 1886, Berlin; he is probably now best remembered for having published the first edition of Georg Büchner's works, thus saving plays such as *Woyzeck* from oblivion.

But it was as a writer of reportage, short stories and novels set in his homeland, the area of East Galicia and the Bukovina, that he became widely known during his lifetime.

One of his main concerns was the depiction of the downtrodden ethnic groups, whether *shtetl* Jews or Slav peasants. His portrayal of the people of this backward area is not at all folksy local colour, but is informed by his deep humanitarian concern for the oppressed and exploited classes and nationalities.

His other focus is on the Jews of the region. As an educated and "enlightened" Jew, he believed the way forward was education and the adoption of the German language and culture. But he was opposed to forcible Germanization (or Polonization) and sympathetic to traditional ways of life. For all his knowledge of local habits and customs which informs his novels, the main emphasis in his work is on the individual.

His best and most important novel is *Der Pojaz*, a *Bildungsroman* about a young Jew who wants to escape ghetto life and become an actor. *Leib Weihnachtskuchen and his Child* (first published in 1896), with its portrayal of a poverty-stricken Jew whose religion is personal and deeply felt, is probably the one with the most immediate appeal for the modern reader. The inevitability with which the tragedy gradually unfolds still has the power to move.

Four of Franzos's works were translated into English and published in Britain and the US in the 1880s. His works are still in print in Germany and he is an important witness to the cultural history of the eastern fringes of the old Habsburg Empire.

The geographical and historical setting

Leib Weihnachtskuchen and his Child is set in East Galicia, nowadays a province, since the collapse of the Soviet Union, of the Ukraine. It lies to the east of Slovakia, beyond the Carpathians, on the River Dniester, between the cities of L'viv and Chernivsty. Occasionally Franzos also uses the term "Podolia", which refers to a larger area of the south-western Ukraine.

In the Middle Ages Galicia-Volhynia was a wealthy principality, which was absorbed into Poland in the fourteenth century (when the rest of the Ukraine was conquered by the Mongols). Following the partitions of Poland in the eighteenth century, it became part of the Habsburg Empire. After the First World War part was given to Poland, part to Rumania; after the Second it was taken over by the Soviet Union; in 1991 it became part of the independent republic of Ukraine.

The majority of the population are Ukrainians. At the time *Leib Weihnachtskuchen* is set, the 1870s or 1880s, the aristocracy and upper classes were largely Polish, and Ukrainians who wanted to "get on" tended to Polonize. The region contained other ethnic groups, including many Jewish communities. The Ukrainian Catholic Church retains the Orthodox rites but is united with Rome.

The Ukrainian language has a common origin with Russian,

but is distinct. For the sake of simplicity, and to emphasize that this was a region where the majority of the population were under the dominion of other peoples, I have retained the German forms for the main towns: Lemberg (Polish Lwów, Russian Lvov, Ukrainian L'viv), Czernowitz (Russian Chernovsty, Ukrainian Chernivsty) and Halicz (in transliteration from Russian it can appear as either Galich or Halich). For the same reason I have also kept the term "Ruthene" used by the Poles and Germans for the Slav peasantry, part, Hessell Tiltman claims in his book *Peasant Europe* (1936), of the denial of Ukrainian identity. In the same spirit the Russians referred to their Ukrainians as "Little Russians".

I would like to thank my friends, Heather and Mike Valencia, for their willing help in all matters Jewish and Yiddish. Any remaining *faux pas* in those areas are all my own work.

Michael Mitchell

1

Anyone travelling by rail from Lemberg to Czernowitz might be forgiven for thinking that East Galicia is less densely populated than it is. Miles of desolate heath or poor farmland, a few cottages in the distance, but rarely a large village. Elsewhere the traveller can often tell from the position of the cottages and the shape of their gardens just how the railway line must have been forced through. Here there is only one place where this can be seen: at the point where the line, heading south-east from the old town of Halicz, which gave its name to the whole province of Galicia, touches the boundary of the village of Vinkovce. On the right is a fine old farmstead, standing at an angle to the railway; on the left its orchard. The iron track has cut a flourishing farm in two.

    The owner of the farm was a Ruthene peasant called Janko Vygoda. It would seem to us a comic name, meaning as it does "John Convenience", but it is so widespread it doesn't strike the locals as the least bit odd. Remembering the drudgery these people's existence consists of, one might imagine it must be a kind of consolation, something to remind them of an easier life. But *vygoda* is also the word for a short cut through the fields which neighbours are permitted to use; *vygoda* then became the name of the land and, when Emperor Joseph introduced surnames, was transferred to its owners. Of course, the decline in prosperity of this class has been so great that nowadays many hundreds bear the name who have not the power to permit or forbid anything to anyone.

Our Janko Vygoda was better off. He still farmed the land his forefathers had farmed, but his life was hard enough. Perhaps it was his ugliness alone that had saved him from ruin. Of all the people in the village, his parents were the merriest, thirstiest and gave least thought to the morrow. Physically they were a type often found among these most pure-blooded of the Slavs who have only a few drops of Mongol blood: tall, strong, corpulent, with curly blond hair and watery blue eyes. And this couple, of all people, had the misfortune to be blessed with a baby exhibiting the dark skin and features of the Mongols. The neighbours grinned. At the baptism even the priest could not resist the old joke of holding the infant under water for a few more seconds that normal, muttering, "The poor little devil certainly needs it." His mother cried and his father comforted her by saying, "Perhaps the Devil will take the changeling back and God will give us a Christian child."

Neither wish was fulfilled. Janko remained their only child and grew into a strong and sinewy, though also short and lean boy with a pale, yellowish complexion and slanting eyes that peered out warily through a mass of coarse black hair. But the most ugly thing about his face was its permanent expression of grim defiance. Neither the neighbours' mockery, nor his mother's scolding nor his father's kicks had managed to make Janko any more cheerful.

More hardworking, though. He stuck to the farmhands, because they did not beat him, and worked tirelessly in the most distant fields, where his father was never seen. The time came, however, when he could work in the orchard beside the house without meeting him. There was too much business that took Hritzko Vygoda away from the farm. In the mornings he had to go and see one of the three moneylenders into whose hands he had fallen: the owner of the Vinkovce estate, Baron Paterski; the Armenian lessee of the Halicz estate, Stefan Kastanasiewicz; and the Jew, Moses Erdkugel, in Halicz. These three men bestowed their blessings at the same rate: fifty, a hundred and, whenever possible, two hundred per cent. Only the worthy Erdkugel had been convicted of usury. And quite rightly so. He carried on his business quite openly, ignoring the consideration due to friendly officials. The Pole and the Armenian did show consideration and were therefore counted men of honour. Hritzko Vygoda preferred to deal with them, and only went to the Jew when needs must. That was his morning occupation. In the afternoon he got drunk in the inn and in the evening Janko had to haul him home with the help of one of the farmhands.

This was the only contact between father and son, and it was peaceful because the old man was blind drunk. Janko never entered the inn as a customer and he was eighteen before the first drop of schnapps passed his lips. Even that occurred against his will. On a scorching hot day he collapsed out in the fields from overwork. The labourers tried to revive him with a mouthful of alcohol, but it was more his loathing of the well-known acrid smell than the fiery taste that brought him round.

However much he cursed his fate, there was one thing he was thankful for: his parents had never taken him with them to the inn because he was so ugly they were ashamed of him. That was good. It allowed him to keep the farm going. True, all his efforts led to nothing, as long as they were alive. His mother neglected the house, his father sold the grain on the stalk and did not buy even the most essential tools. But given their way of life, they were bound to die soon. As a child he had hated them as long as he was afraid of them; as a youth he lived alongside them, detached, indifferent. He did not wish them an early death, but it was bound to come, as surely as winter follows autumn.

Then he would be the master and all would be well. That in fact all would not not well, that not one blade of grass, not one ear of corn belonged to his father any more, but to the three aforementioned benefactors, was well-known to several people in the village, but not to the one most closely concerned. His father owed the usurers money and it would have to be repaid, that he knew, but not that things were even worse. And who would have told him? He had no friends and kept his intercourse with the villagers to the bare minimum. The people mocked him, calling him a changeling, a sourpuss. His life consisted of nothing but work and there may have been some who felt sorry for him, but all avoided him wherever possible. His farmhands did the same. As a master he was just, not asking more of others than of himself, but still they breathed a sigh of relief when he went on his way. Janko, for his part, was completely indifferent to the other villagers, apart from one, whom he hated with a bitter hatred: the tenant of the village inn, Leib Weihnachtskuchen.

Leib "Christmascake": another odd name, and not the only one, either. It, like other, similar names can be explained by the fact that the officials who imposed them on the Jews of the country were witty gentlemen. But Leib's grandfather was not concerned about the name, and he himself had other things to worry about. A tiny, pathetic, crumpled scrap of humanity, he crept round with a timid, humbly beseeching expression on his face, as if he were asking everyone he met, "You don't object to Leib Weihnachtskuchen being alive, do you?"

No village innkeeper in Podolia takes it amiss if his customers call him "Jewish dogshit" and tweak his sidelocks. If necessary, Leib would put up with much worse. But that happened rarely. On the contrary, he was treated better by his regulars than most other innkeepers. In the first place he was so frail they felt sorry for him. Secondly there was no reason to be jealous of him. He was as poor as the least farm labourer in Vinkovce, and he and his wife and child went hungry more often than they filled their bellies. The lease was in his name, true, but Baron Paterski, to whom the inn belonged, had dispensed with a deposit "because he felt sorry for him", and Moses Erdkugel had paid for the stock; now the two had him in their clutches for good. Lastly he was so stupid, if he hadn't been a Jew they would have assumed he was honest. He didn't water his schnapps, didn't chalk things up twice, didn't encourage anyone to drink and if someone asked him to arrange a loan from his own two benefactors, he would even advise against it—though in vain in the case of Hritzko. No, they left Leib in peace.

Only Janko hated him, with a burning hatred. For him this tiny man embodied the twin destroyers of his parents: schnapps and usury. Leib was aware of this and when the young man came to the inn in the evening, to collect his drunken father, he would greet him shyly then slip into a dark corner; outside, he kept well out of his way. Once there was no room and he was to suffer for it.

It happened one cold, foggy November day on the short cut, the *vygoda* that had given Janko's family their name. Teeth chattering in his thin, patched caftan, little Leib was hurrying along the narrow path, which followed an embankment. Either side were marshy meadows that were only used as pasture in the middle of summer. Now they were under water which was already showing the first thin layer of ice. Suddenly the silhouette of a man approaching appeared through the mist. He recognized his deadly enemy and stood still, trembling. "Out of my way," shouted Janko, "the *vygoda's* not for Jews," and he raised his fist. Trying to avoid the blow, Leib stumbled and fell down the slope. The cover of ice gave way under him. "Help!" he cried, in fear of his life, but Janko continued on his way; a dog he would have helped, but not Leib Weihnachtskuchen. "Help!" came the second cry, already fainter. The young man stopped, his heart was starting to thump, but then he continued on his way. He won't die, he thought, the water's too shallow. And if he should, did I throw him in? But by now his heart was pounding so painfully against his ribs he felt constrained to stop.

He looked back. It was already getting dark, the fog was thickening and there was no sound other than the creak of the ice in the marsh. There it was again! No more than a rasping groan that sounded as if it came from a great distance, but still he heard it clearly: "Help!" He hurried back. As he was approaching the spot, he heard other voices. Two men from the village were dragging Leib up the embankment. "Is he dead?" asked Janko. "Probably," replied one, the other adding, in sympathetic tones, "Who can have pushed the poor little dogshit down? He's never done anyone any harm."

Leib was not dead, but for several weeks he lay in a fever, half way between life and death. His delirious ramblings revealed how the accident had happened. His parents, indeed all the villagers heaped reproaches on Janko, but he was unmoved. "Did I throw him in?" was his initial response, and then not even that.

But there was something that did make an impression on him: the way the Jew's wife looked at him when he came into the inn in the evening. The pale, careworn woman, old before her time, did not say a word, but her despairing, menacing look sent shivers down his spine. Even worse, however, were the times during the day when he saw little blond-haired Miriam, the innkeeper's only daughter, sitting outside the house. Normally so cheerful, now she just sat there, her head hanging sorrowfully.

It was this above all that led Janko to a decision he found difficult to take. After the Jew, the priest was the man he hated most in the village. If the joke he had made at his christening was not enough, Father Jephrem was drunk by midday every day. But Janko went to him with two twenty-kreutzer coins and ordered a mass for "the life of a sick man".

"Fine," said Father Jephrem, "he's as good as recovered."

"Even if he's a Jew?" asked Janko.

"No!" exclaimed the priest, but immediately thought better of it. "In that case," he went on, "it'll take longer, d'you understand? Naturally. And it'll cost you three twenty-kreutzer pieces."

The priest was quite correct. Leib Weihnachtskuchen recovered, only it took quite a long time.

When Janko heard that Leib was back in the taproom of the inn, he avoided meeting him and sent the farmhands to collect his father. What's the point? he thought. It'll only lead to argument. And the things he'll say about me to all the others!

But what actually happened was different, so very different that at first Janko could not believe it. People came up to him, one after the other, and said, "Hey, Janko, I was wrong. Leibko says it wasn't your fault at all." Even Hritzko confirmed it, in his own inimitable way. "You go round looking as if you've swallowed a load of cowshit, you ugly changeling," he growled, "you begrudge your poor old father a little schnapps now and then, but at least you're not a murderer…"

How can that be, thought Janko, the Jew's telling lies to make me look good. There must be something behind it. So one morning, as he was passing the inn, he gave way to a strange, mixed feeling, part defiance, part remorse, part gratitude, and went in.

He was somewhat pale as he entered, but the Jew went even paler when he saw him. Then, in a quivering voice, he asked if perhaps Pan Janko had come to take a glass of something.

"I don't need your poison," the latter exclaimed. "What I do want is to know why you're telling these lies. You ducked to avoid my fist. I was responsible for your accident."

"But why—?" asked the Jew, timidly. "I'm sorry, Pan Janko, but it was meant for the best."

"Exactly! I don't deserve it."

Only now did Leib Weihnachtskuchen understand what had got into Janko. "Let me worry about that," he said, with his sad, humble smile. Janko had to press him to get an explanation. "It's not so easy to say. In the first place, what's the point of taking revenge on you? Do I get anything out of it? Would it cancel out the six weeks I was ill? Would it make me any healthier than I am? And then, who am I? A poor, weak Yid. And you're a big, strong Christian. You hate me anyway, should I provoke you so you knock me down and kill me? You'd end up in prison, Pan Janko, but that wouldn't feed my wife and child. But it wasn't just that I was afraid…" He hesitated. "You won't get angry if I tell you?"

"No. Go on, tell me." Without realising it, young Janko had stopped addressing the Jew in the familiar form he used for children and animals.

"It was…well…I've not been blessed by fortune, Pan Janko, a hand-to-mouth existence and everyone tramples on me…but I still have my wife and my Miriam…. And I know one person in the village who—"

"You're wrong there!" the young man broke in angrily, despite his promise. "I don't need your pity," he went on, "I'll get our farm back on its feet again, eventually."

The Jew shook his head. "That you won't, Pan Janko," he said.

"Why not?" Janko cried. "Because you pour too many schnapps for my father and pocket too many fees for arranging loans in Halicz?"

The little Jew drew back and his pale face flushed. "As God is my witness," he cried, "you do me an injustice. I have never encouraged people to drink, always tried to stop them from having too much. I sell schnapps, arrange deals, yes, that's my business. If I didn't, someone else would. And then, money and schnapps, both poison, you say, they destroy people, you say. But in that case that knife in your belt's a poison too, you could cut your throat with it. You use it to cut your bread, that's good—but even if you cut your throat with it, the knife would not be guilty of your death. Of course, money, schnapps, knives, they're all dangerous. But why am I going on like this, you don't understand what I'm getting at?"

No, Janko could not understand him, at least not entirely. But one thing he did understand: he had done this man an injustice. "Hmm...that bit about the knife..." he mumbled in embarrassment. Then he asked, "But tell me, why do you think I'll never get our farm back on its feet again?"

The Jew shrugged his shoulders. "What do I know?" he muttered. "Is it my farm? Maybe I'm wrong." That was all Janko could get out of him.

For the time being, anyway. Gradually things changed, though. Janko came back, again and again, until during the next winter he was to be found almost daily in the inn. The people were amazed, since he still never touched a drop. Even less could they understand why Leib wasted his time with a man out of whom there was no profit to be made.

There were times when even the Jew himself could not understand it. Janko went to see him because he had gradually come to understand the metaphor of the knife, because he had discarded the hatred that had obsessed him from his childhood days, and because from Leib he learnt what his true situation was and could ask for advice as to how the ruin of his hopes might yet be averted. But Leib? "Perhaps I'll be able to do some business with him some day," he would say, to reassure both himself and his wife, for he knew that as soon as his father died, Janko would be a pauper. Since his wife had died, Hritzko's drinking had been even worse, if that were possible. The truth—that he put up with Janko out of pity—was something Leib Weihnachtskuchen was not keen to admit even to himself. Could he, poor as he was, afford to squander so much time? He preferred to think up another reason, which at least had the advantage of being true: "He's so nice to the child." And indeed, little Miriam, who at the time was ten years old, was the only creature capable of bringing a smile to the sullen Ruthene's lips. He would spend weeks making her some new toy with his clumsy hands, since he did not have the money to buy one. "Just until I can afford to buy you one," he would say, and Leib would smile his good-natured smile. But what he thought was, "Not on earth, perhaps in a better world."

Next spring—young Janko was twenty-one—Hritzko died where he had lived, in the inn. The three usurers called in their debts, a date was set for the sale and the only matter unresolved was which of the three would get the farm. In vain Leib went on Janko's behalf from the nobleman to the Armenian, from the Armenian to the Jew, begging them to grant him a stay of execution.

Then the miracle happened. One day the worst of the three, Baron Paterski, did not throw the Jew out, as was his wont, but gave him a hearing and said, "If this Janko really is as hardworking as you say, it might be worth giving him a try. Send him to me." No one in Vinkovce had ever covered the distance from the estate office to the village as quickly as Leib Weihnachtskuchen on his short, bandy legs.

Janko was dazed by this unexpected piece of good fortune. When Paterski said, "Good, I'll try to keep the farm together for you," he was filled with joy, perhaps for the first time in his life.

The miracle, however, turned out to have a very natural explanation when Paterski stated his conditions. His intention was clearly to save himself the legal costs of arranging the sale and get the land improved at no expense to himself. The interest and amortization rates he insisted on were so high that no one could see them being covered by the yield from the run-down farm. If Janko missed one single instalment, all would be lost.

The young peasant did not understand this, but the Jew

certainly did. Distraught, he padded up and down; then he went and begged Janko not to sign.

"I'm a fool advising you against it," he moaned. "Paterski's promised me three crowns if the business goes through, and you'll give me at least two. Five crowns, that's a fortune. And if you don't sign, he says he'll throw me out of the inn. But it was that that opened my eyes. Go away and find work as a labourer on someone else's farm. You're hardworking, you'll be well paid, perhaps you'll even marry the farmer's daughter—though perhaps not, given your ugly face. But anything's better than this contract. Let God do as He likes with me. If He's turned me into such a fool, He'll have to take care of me somehow or other."

But Janko insisted he'd manage somehow. He didn't want to go away to people he didn't know.

"Because the people here like you so much?!" the old Jew exclaimed. "Who've you got here?"

"My birthright! And you. And then...I've just got used to it, you see...I feel there's something missing when I don't hear your daughter laughing."

"Oh you fool!" Leib exclaimed. But little Miriam came rushing out of the corner, the tears pouring down her normally happy face. "Stay here, Janko," she cried, sobbing, "I like you. And no one else plays with me."

And so the contract was signed.

But it was also kept. Month after month Leib was given the repayment to take to Paterski. But the Baron was becoming suspicious. "It seems to me," he said, "you must be getting it from the Armenian, or Moses Erdkugel. Those wretches are trying to do me down by lending at ninety per cent."

He was wrong, Janko found the money himself. Good harvests helped, but cost him an incredible effort. No labourer would have put up with the food he ate, the clothes he wore. Even the shack was rented out to the assistant Father Jephrem had to pay for because by now he was only sober very early in the morning. Summer and winter, Janko slept in the cowshed. And no one in Vinkovce had ever worked so hard. He rose with the hens in the morning and it was late at night before he collapsed onto his miserable pallet. "Our dogs have a better life," the neighbours said contemptuously, for what he was doing seemed to them not only unworthy of the owner of a farm, but also foolish. How could a man think he could escape his fate? Only a few felt sorry for him, sometimes wondering how anyone could put up with a life like that.

If that came to Janko's ears, he merely smiled. He had become accustomed to the hard work and privations, just as others get used to riotous living, and his life was not without its little pleasures. He had one good hour each day, the hour between eleven and twelve when all work stops in East Galicia and they have their midday meal. Janko sat in the inn, ate his bread, washed it down with water and chatted to Leib and Miriam. He had stopped bringing her toys; he no longer had the time to make them, nor she to play with them. Now she was twelve she had to help her mother with the housework. But she still laughed as much as ever, and the gloomy expression on Janko's face brightened whenever he heard her laughter. Occasionally he even thought up a joke to amuse her. Even he was surprised that it happened, but it did. Miriam could get him to do anything, even to treat himself to some meat or a new jerkin, but she only did that when she knew that the money for the next instalment was safely tucked away.

Perhaps it was that hour that gave him the strength to keep up the payments, right down to the very last heller, until a whole sixth had been paid off. Now even Leib began to hope. His wife's health was growing steadily worse, she was visibly wasting away with consumption; his own plight and worries were threatening to overwhelm him, but he still found time to concern himself with Janko.

"It was criminal of me," he told him, "not to have made a greater effort to dissuade you five years ago, but I think the time has come when I can ease my conscience a little. Now that what you owe Paterski is a little less than what your farm is worth, I'm sure we can find a decent man who'll get you out of his clutches and take lower interest."

And a decent man was indeed found, the parish priest of Solince, who was none other than the father of the assistant priest lodging with Janko. Partly because it seemed a secure investment and partly because of the good things his son had to say about his landlord, he took over the loan at a mere twenty per cent. Not at all extortionate for Galicia.

Of course, Baron Paterski realized who had ruined his profitable arrangement. "Just you wait, Weihnachtskuchen," he barked at the little Jew the next time they met, "I'll bake you a New Year's cake that'll stick in your craw and choke you to death."

Alarmed, Leib hurried home, but he soon recovered his composure. He even made a little joke about it to his wife, though the joke was as thin and feeble as he was: "He'll renew the lease, surely, he wouldn't be able to pull as many plums out of another man as he can out of this Christmas cake. And it's four months till New Year."

"You sacrifice yourself for that Janko," his wife complained. "You don't think of me and the child." Leib was silent for a while, letting the storm blow over, then he said hesitantly, "Who knows, perhaps that farmer might put some nice business my way one of these days."

"And how is he going to do that?" she cried.

Silence was his only reply. How? was a mystery to him too.

2

A few weeks later this conversation was repeated. It was a Monday morning and Chane had been counting the number of glasses that had been marked up on the slate behind the bar the previous day. The sum total was an impressive demonstration of the thirst of the good people of Vinkovce. And they had taken three crowns in cash as well. "We might have been able to make a go of it," she moaned, "and now we're going to be thrown out because of that Janko."

Leib tried to reassure her. "I expect Paterski'll let us stay here after all," he said. "Another man wouldn't put up with the kind of things I do. And as for Janko, well…"

"Well?" she snapped impatiently, when he paused.

"He's twenty-six," he said timidly, "he's hardworking and the farm's big. You just wait and see, Chane, it'll bring us ten crowns."

"Not ten kreutzers!" she cried. "There isn't an unmarried woman around who's so old and ugly she'd take that scarecrow. You know that yourself. You go to all that trouble for him out of the goodness of your heart. You're only deceiving yourself and me if you think it's going to bring in some profit for us."

Leib was silent for a while, embarrassed as he always was when the devious workings of his mind were laid bare, but then he made an effort to contradict his wife.

She cut him short. "Nonsense! If you've so much time to spare, why don't you look for a husband for our Miriam."

Leib Weihnachtkuchen's jaw dropped and his eyes opened wide. "What—what are you thinking of?" he mumbled in consternation. "She's still only a child."

"She's nearly sixteen," Chane countered. "You just have a look at her," she said, pointing out into the yard where Miriam was hanging out the washing.

He looked in the direction she was pointing, and the longer he looked the more fixed his gaze became. Then he gave a deep sigh.

"Well?" Chane asked impatiently.

But no answer came from Leib. The sudden shock had left him speechless. And yet it was a beautiful picture that presented itself to his eye: an innocent girl, full of vigour, a bud swelling into blossom. But that was just it! The way she was standing there, on her toes, her thin dress tucked up, revealing the strong curve of her leg, the way her body leant backwards, her hands reached up to the line, making the coarse cloth of her bodice stretch tight over her young, rounded breasts—was that the same little Miriam his eye had been used to seeing over all these years?! It must have happened overnight, was the thought that went through his mind. It never occurred to him that the fault lay in his eyes. Those dull eyes that were always on the lookout for a piece of bread, those poor eyes so quick to close when a punch threatened, had not been open to the fairest, most natural miracle that was unfolding before them.

"What are you staring like that for?" Chane snapped at him. "You know what she looks like."

His only answer was another deep sigh. Yes, now he knew. And when the girl out in the yard stood up on tiptoe again to hang up the next wet shirt, once more emphasising every line of her young body, a blush spread over the little man's grey, wrinkled face. "Chane," he stammered, "she ought to…ought to put on a jacket and…and not tuck her dress up like that," he added, embarrassed.

"Old fool!" she snorted. "Is that all you've got to say? D'you want she should hang out the washing in an ankle-length gown? What's wrong if anyone does see that it's pleased God—praised be His name—to let her grow so into such a lovely, plump, heavy girl." She was interrupted by one of her nasty fits of coughing and it was quite a while before she could continue. "The only harm is if she's not seen by the right people, couples with a nice boy. Why don't you do something about that?"

Fortunately for the little man, the conversation was interrupted. A farmer had come into the taproom and Chane went to serve him, leaving Leib in the bedroom, with its window out into the yard, trying to order the thoughts that were whirling round in his head. If only he could stop himself looking at his daughter! He could not get used to the sight and it disturbed him.

No longer a child! At first that was all he could think of. Then a tiny spark of pride and happiness ignited and spread its warmth through his bitter, downtrodden heart. Chane was right, they should thank God Miriam had turned out like this, not just healthy, but a big, bonny lass. Not obese, though, not the kind of tub of lard where a father would say, "My son couldn't afford to feed her in the manner she's been accustomed to," but juicy, like a pear that has just ripened, and with such power in her limbs that any blade of grass her bare foot trod on in the yard—he could see it clearly—did not stand up again, but stayed crushed to the ground.

"A heavy girl." That was the ideal of beauty this people had brought with them—along with many other things that both inspired them and dragged them down—from the hot, faraway homeland that was lost for ever. Miriam was plump, "heavy", and that made her beautiful, but when Leib now looked at her face, scrutinising it as closely as if he were seeing it for the first time, he was clearly delighted by it too. He closed his eyes and rocked his head from side to side. A proud smile lit up his pale, thin lips, raising the corners of the mouth that were normally turned down. Even a less prejudiced judge would have taken pleasure in the fresh, round face. True, the features were somewhat coarse, but they were well-formed: an obstinate chin jutting out under the strong red mouth; a gently curving nose; big, round, brown eyes sparkling with innocent fire and merriment; and a wealth of auburn curls round her low forehead, which resisted being bound in plaits and which the sunlight wove into a shimmering, swaying halo round her head. That light reddish gold is very rare among the Jewish women of Eastern Europe. If they have fair hair, then it is usually pale blond or gingery. But the shape of her nose and her fiery eyes clearly showed which blood ran in Miriam's veins.

Her delighted father did not see that. On the contrary, the thought that went through his mind was: She doesn't look like a Jewish girl at all! and the corners of his mouth rose even higher. And who would blame the poor man for this weakness when everything he had experienced throughout his life had inscribed on his brain with strokes of the lash the idea that "looking Jewish" was a misfortune, a guarantee of endless suffering and scorn. And then he remembered what old David Münzer, the rich owner of the sawmill in Halicz, had said a few days ago. The sun was beating down and he had stopped outside the inn to refresh himself with a glass of the vinegary Moldavian wine. Miriam had brought it and he had smiled as he said, "You would only find a girl like that in a country village."

Baron Paterski, too, had once called out to him, "Leibko, your Chane must have been unfaithful. That can't be your daughter." Leib had assumed it was one of the noble gentleman's jokes—at that time, before he had arranged the deal between Janko and the priest of Solince, his lordship occasionally favoured him with a joke—but now he realized what Paterski was saying. He gave a contented nod. He no more thought Chane had been unfaithful than he thought the sun had ever fallen out of the sky. His only conclusion was that even the nobleman had noticed his daughter's "Christian" looks.

In this he was mistaken, of course. All Paterski was doing, in his crude way, was to express his astonishment that such a frail couple should have such a strapping child. But Chane too had once been the picture of health, only to wither quickly under the burden of care after a too-early marriage. The full vigour of this race, whose capacity for endurance would be unparalleled if its misfortune were not almost equally great, appears mostly in its women. The young Jewish men of the east are small, weakly, pigeon-chested, just the way their circumstances have made them, but the young women are strong, overflowing with energy, a mystery amid the reek and grime of the despised poverty of the lowest of the low. At the same time each and every one of these women is a solution to the mystery of how this people has managed to survive all its immense hardships.

What was that?! Little Leib started. Now she was singing as she worked. Her high voice rang out in the autumn sunshine:

> Janko, don't come here again,
> Father's warned me about men,
> Mother's always nagging too,
> Telling me the things they do.

He knew the song, every girl in the village sang it. He'd often heard Miriam sing it before, without seeing any harm in it, even though the next verse was not entirely suitable for an innocent girl's lips. But now it struck him: she's singing just like a Christian girl! And it wasn't a pleasurable thought this time. But Chane appeared in the doorway and called out in a sharp voice, "What did I tell you on Friday, Miriam? You're not to sing any more now. You're too big now."

And when the girl obediently stopped, she turned to her husband. "Are you still sitting here? Why don't you find yourself something useful to do or—" she lowered her voice so that Miriam couldn't hear "—go to Halicz and talk to Mendele Shadchen?"

"All right, all right," said the little man, looking for his stick and hat, "I'll go to Halicz, I've got business there anyway. But I should talk to Mendele?"

"Who else?" she said scornfully. "To the priest? That's Mendele's business. By the time you find a son-in-law she'll be going grey. Almost sixteen! It's high time something was done."

"You're right," he said in conciliatory tones. "It was just that Mendele costs so much…. What should I say to him?"

"What should you say to him?! That you want to buy an estate on the moon!" But then she let out a deep sigh and sank into a chair, a dejected look on her face. "Mendele will ask about the dowry, of course. And we've got nothing. We can't even offer to take in our son-in-law for a few years, Paterski will give us notice to quit at New Year. Next summer we'll be beggars ourselves."

"He won't give us notice to quit," said Leib comfortingly. "And even if he does, we'll find another inn to lease."

When, at this, Chane shook her head as the tears suddenly came pouring down her withered cheeks, he took her hand and said, in almost reverent tones, "Remember what He can do. He can do more than find a new inn for little Leib."

"All for the sake of an ugly peasant!" Her voice was so choked with tears of fury that her vehement exclamation was scarcely comprehensible.

Leib tried to smile. "Well, yes," he said hesitantly, "Janko's certainly ugly, and he's a peasant too.... But," he went on, and a kind of radiance appeared on his careworn features as his voice gradually became stronger, "I didn't do it for Janko's sake, but for His sake. Has He not commanded us: Love thy neighbour as thyself, even if he is a stranger? And for my own sake, too. You know I don't ask much for myself, no more than others... everyone pushes me around, everyone, even you, Chane—you're usually right of course—even you are often unhappy with me.... But there is one thing I insist on."

She stopped crying and looked up. His voice had a strange richness to it, such as she had hardly ever heard before. "What do you mean?" she murmured.

"That He is happy with me and that I can look Him in the eye. When I stand there in the morning"—he pointed to the window that faced east—"with the *tefillin* on my forehead and left arm, and the sun rises over Halicz and looks in at the window, then I always feel that He is looking at me, looking through me, right into my heart of hearts. And as my lips whisper the prayers, my heart is saying, 'Here I am, Eternal Lord, a sorely tried man and the least of Your servants, but whatever is in my power to do, that Your name be hallowed on earth by the fulfilment of Your will, that shall be done.' And it was so that I could still say that, that I arranged the business between Janko and the priest of Solince. Do you think He doesn't know about that? Perhaps He will let us be ruined after all, His ways are unfathomable. But until that happens, I will continue to hope for His mercy. Be comforted, woman, He will send us bread and an honest son-in-law."

With that he put his hat on—his head was shaven, according to the custom of the strict Jews, protected just by a faded skullcap—and took up his walking stick. "Goodbye. I will be back by the evening."

"Just one word," she said.

"About Him?" he asked, raising his hands to ward off any suggestion of criticism.

"No. My father used to say, 'If you're sensible and help yourself, then God will help you too.' And my father was a devout Jew. But there's something else I have to say. You can tell Mendele we intend to have our son-in-law, the young couple, live with us for a few years, and to provide for the little children, if God should send some. But that mustn't be the main point. In the first place everything's uncertain at the moment, and even if things do turn out all right, it'll be hard to find a strong, decent, devout boy who will be willing to take on such poverty. A boy like that, who's willing to make do with board and lodgings as a dowry, will easily find something better—"

"But not a girl like that," Leib interjected.

"Are we Christians?" she replied. "Do we marry for beauty? Do we marry for 'love'? If a girl's well brought up and healthy, we don't ask if she has a pretty face. That's why the important thing is to ask Mendele if he doesn't know of someone who would have no chance of getting a girl with a dowry. I'm thinking of a widower with lots of children, or a man who needs looking after…"

Leib staggered back as if he had been hit. "Chane!" he cried. "Our lovely child?!"

"Do you imagine I find it easy?" she said, her lips twitching. "But what do you think is the greater sin against God: to give her to a man like that, or to let her remain unmarried? And what is the greater misfortune: to be provided for by a man like that, or to go round begging with us? So that's what you have to tell Mendele…. It doesn't have to be today," she added when she saw how pale he had gone, "but it has to be done. Do you hear?"

He just nodded. Eventually he muttered, "If that's so, then better today than tomorrow," and hurried off on his bandy legs.

But not for long. Once the last houses of the village were behind him and he was in the little wood beside the road to Halicz, he trudged along more and more slowly and the head with the straggly grey beard sank lower and lower onto his chest. Finally he stopped, looked round furtively, as if he were about some secret business, and slipped into the trees. There he sank down onto the roots of a beech tree and began to cry, to cry so that the tears poured down his furrowed cheeks in torrents.

That was rare. He had not cried for years and years, not since that day fifteen years ago when his only son had been buried. The little boy was just two years old, he had not yet learnt to talk, but his death had been a sword-thrust to Leib's heart, for the doctor had told him his wife could have no more children. To have just a daughter and no son to continue the line, to mark the *yahrzeit*, the anniversary of his parents' death, with his prayers, is the deepest sorrow a devout Jew has to bear. He had never thought such a sorrow could be his lot, and now it had happened…

Leib Weihnachtskuchen rarely cried and for that reason the tears soothed his aching heart once again, just as they had after his son's funeral. Only this time he was racked by a double anguish. It was not just the danger to his beloved daughter that was tormenting him, even more distressing was the fact that he was condemned to be the instrument that brought it down on her. But perhaps He would spare him this, the danger was not yet upon them…

He undid the frayed strip of black cloth he used as a belt to hold his caftan together and dried his eyes on it. He could not see that the dye came out of the cloth and left grotesque black streaks on the wrinkled skin of his flushed face. Now that his grief had relieved itself in tears, he sat there under the beech tree for a long time. An occasional belated tear ran down and he quickly wiped it away, turning the black smudges into strange figures on his forehead and cheeks. It was at this point that a thought suddenly struck him. What an ass I was to be pleased she doesn't look Jewish! What use is that to her? Should she marry a Christian? Would it lighten the heavy burden she'll have to carry through life by one single ounce? Would it have lightened my load? Even if my legs had been as straight as my stick and I'd had a face like cavalry lieutenant, a Yid's a Yid, they'd still have beaten me.

The tears stopped and a sigh escaped him from time to time, until eventually his smile returned. Fool that I am, he thought as he slowly went on his way, why am I worrying? He ordains everything differently from the way we short-sighted humans imagine they will be. If anyone had told me yesterday I would be going to Halicz today to find a husband for my little Miriam, I'd have told them they were mad. And that's what I'm doing! So what is the point of agonising over whom He has destined to be my son-in-law?

He started to step out, but then another thought brought him to a halt. I'm going to Halicz anyway, I have to borrow twenty crowns for Onufrij the blacksmith. But to see Mendele?...Didn't Chane say it doesn't have to be today? But why not today? I'll just chat to him, about things in general, not a word about what she calls the main point. There's still plenty of time for that and I hope—I put my trust in Him to provide for us.

Now he hurried on, more quickly than usual. Soon the wood was behind him and he could see ahead the red wooden cross by the well that marked the boundary between Vinkovce and Halicz. He had almost reached the well when he heard his name called from far off.

He looked up. It was Janko. The fields by the boundary belonged to him and he was ploughing for the winter corn. A boy was leading the oxen, Janko was walking beside the plough. Without stopping work, he waved the little man over.

Leib headed across the stubble, but when he came near the team, the boy's eyes opened wide in astonishment and he broke out into roars of laughter. Even the gloomy Janko's lips twitched.

But then he hurried over to Leib. "Hey!" he cried. "What have you been up to? Those marks on your face?"

The boy was still roaring with uncontrollable laughter, but Janko suddenly looked worried. "You've been crying... . For heaven's sake—has something—at home—?" He could hardly speak and grasped the little Jew's hand.

Leib tried to smile, but all his thin lips could manage was an embarrassed grin. "God forbid. Should something have happened?...And crying? Why should I cry? But this wind"—there had not been a breath all day—"old eyes, you know, they easily water." He passed his hand over his face and looked at it in astonishment. It was black. "The dust..."

Janko shook his head. "Turn," he ordered the boy, who had laughed until the tears ran down his cheeks. He took his smock off the oxen and added, "We'll start again from the top."

Once the boy had gone, he took Leib by the arm and led him to the well.

"Now wash yourself." Leib did so.

"Good. Now dry yourself." He held out his smock to him, inside out.

Leib declined the offer. "No, the water will dry off in the air...it'll make your smock dirty."

But Janko insisted. "Otherwise you won't get rid of the marks. You're going to Halicz... . Anyway, it's a year since it was washed," he added to encourage him.

The Jew complied and said, "I suppose you need something in Halicz. Out with it it, then, I haven't much time."

But Janko held him there. "No," he said, and his little black eyes fixed themselves on the innkeeper's. "I called out to you because of the way you were hurrying along. I thought perhaps Miriam's ill, or your wife. But that's not it? Or is Paterski throwing you out now and you're going to ask your people for advice?...Not that either?...So what is it?"

"But if I tell you it's nothing..."

"You'd be lying." The farmer forced the little Jew onto the bench by the well and sat down beside him. "I know you. You didn't even cry that time when I..."

Though he could not say why, the scene on the *vygoda* had come back to him. As it appeared before his mind's eye, he was overcome with a feeling which never left him, though he kept it well hidden deep down inside: the only man to whom he had done ill was the only man who had been good to him. His heart softened, something that otherwise only happened with the "child", and even there he tried to conceal it.

"Come on, Leibko, old friend," he said, gently stroking the sleeve of his caftan, "you've always been good to me…and I tell you everything, don't I?"

His tone was so unusual that even the little Jew was moved. He was still slightly reluctant to tell him, but only because he thought, he may mean well, this peasant, but he won't understand. What will he say? She's just sixteen and you're in such a hurry? Wait a year, or a few years, until the right man turns up. Eventually, however, he decided to tell him. "All right, Janko, since you put it like that…. But Miriam mustn't hear a word of it."

The young man flushed bright red. "So it is about her?" He brought the words out with difficulty and his slanting eyes narrowed, as if he were expecting a blow.

"Yes. But not a word, Janko, you promise? Not even in teasing, the way you two go on at each other? I have your word?"

"Yes…get on with it."

He was clutching Leib's arm, but the Jew was too immersed in his own thoughts to notice how agitated the other was. "You seem to think there's some great news," he said, making light of it, at the same time drawing a star of David in the sand with his stick. "You're going to be disappointed. It's one of those things that happen all the time. You see—old fool that I am, I never noticed, really I didn't—but of course everyone else did. You see, our little Miriam isn't a little girl any more. Is she, Janko?"

The young Ruthene said nothing. He sat there, motionless, his head leant back against the wooden cross, mouth half open, breathing heavily. The colour had gone from his cheeks, even his lips were pale, and his eyes were still narrowed, as if he could see a weapon descending with deadly force.

"Of course you've noticed," the little Jew went on. "A beautiful girl, a plump, heavy girl"—his smile was a combination of pride and embarrassment—"and for a girl like that..."

"Well?" It sounded like a groan.

"You can still ask? For a girl like that you find a husband."

For a while nothing was said.

"Yes, yes, Janko, my friend," said the old man, "that was what I was on my way—"

He did not get any farther. From deep within the peasant's breast came such a wild, agonized cry that the Jew started in horror, a horror which intensified when he saw how deathly pale, how contorted the young man's face was. His eyes were staring, his mouth hanging open, the corners drawn down. He's dying, was the thought that seized Leib.

"Janko!" he exclaimed, grasping the young Ruthene's hand. It was icy cold, like the hand of a dead man. "What's wrong? Are you ill?" A sudden convulsion, he thought, and looked round for help. In the distance the boy appeared, guiding the plough. Leib waved to him.

"Don't," the young man muttered hoarsely. "Listen..." His voice sank to a wheezing, almost inaudible whisper. "It cannot be."

"What?" the Jew asked apprehensively. He's out of his mind,

he thought, a sudden fever. Once more he looked round for the boy.

Janko straightened up. With a trembling hand he tore open his shirt collar, as if he were suffocating, revealing a brown, matted chest that was rising and falling convulsively as he fought for breath. Finally he had his breath back.

"I won't have it!" he cried in a loud, despairing voice. His eyes, suddenly ablaze with fire, fixed on the Jew. "I'd sooner kill her—myself—all of you.... Don't," he repeated in fury as Leib anxiously started to look round for the ploughboy again. "I'm not mad, no, not any more. I was, though—all that time—it never occurred to me—how things might turn out. But now..." Leib was trembling as Janko grasped his hand in a grip of steel and pulled the little man down onto the bench beside him. "Hear what I have to say, Leibko, for the love of God, hear what I have to say. Between friends, Leibko, between friends. I'm not mad, I'm not threatening you—forget what I said just now. God, I'd rather die ten times over than harm a hair of her head. But it mustn't happen...don't you understand...it would be a disaster for her as well."

Leib Weihnachtskuchen probably did not hear those last words. He sat there, horror-struck, as if a bolt of lightning had just landed in front of him, incapable of movement, incapable of thought. Only a minute ago he would sooner have believed that the grass in the meadows was blue, not green, than that this farmer desired his daughter Miriam. Even Janko's frighteningly odd behaviour had left him unsuspecting. How else could it be? A Ruthene peasant and a Jewish girl?! It just didn't happen, it was against nature!

"God of mercy!" he groaned, closed his eyes and, quivering,

stretched out his hands, as he would have done if a ghost, a dead man whose burial he had attended himself, had appeared to him in broad daylight. God is our only protection against that, only God can save a poor mortal from going out of his mind.

"Don't take on so," Janko said. "Is it that terrible? It just came out like that. I don't know what to say.... There is just one thing I do know: it cannot be. When I think that she won't be in the village any more, will belong to another…oh!"

He groaned. "I beg you," he added in desperation, almost shouting out the words, "please ask her yourself."

"God of mer—" The old man's trembling lips could not even complete the appeal. But the consternation that Janko's last words aroused in him shook him out of his paralysis. Like a drowning man, he fought against the wave of horror that threatened to engulf him. His actions, too, were those of a drowning man. He leapt to his feet and waved his arms about wildly.

"Janko!" he cried, "Have you—?"

He swayed, his lips trembling convulsively, as if they refused to pronounce the terrible word.

The Ruthene stared at him. Then he flushed bright red. "No!" he exclaimed.

"You can swear to it? By…by Him up there?" His eyes were on the ground, but his trembling hand was pointing at the figure of the crucified Christ over the well.

Janko solemnly raised his thumb, index and middle finger. "I swear," he said.

The Jew gave a deep sigh of relief. I must have been mad, he thought. Forgive me, Lord—and you, my child. But it's just one thing after another today.

He passed his hand over his brow and sat down; his legs were still trembling too much to support him. "But why," he asked, "do you want us to ask her? Do you imagine she thinks of you in the same way as you think of her? I'm convinced that's not true."

Janko nodded. "You may well be right," he said gloomily. "She's still a child, has no thought for me—nor for any other man. But I believe that's why she would say no. She's still young, attached to the two of you. What gave you the idea so suddenly? Have you already promised her to someone?" he added anxiously, taking the Jew's hand.

Little Leib hesitated. Perhaps the best thing would be to say yes, he thought. He'll throw a fit, and when it's over, that'll be the end of it. Despite that he said, "No." He couldn't bring himself to lie and he was also concerned at the thought that Janko might start going on at Miriam before he and Chane had had the chance to prepare her.

"No," he repeated, "she's not promised to anyone yet. But we have to talk sensibly about this, Janko." He rested his forehead on his hand. "You see, I still can't really understand; I'd never have thought it of you. How did it happen?"

Janko stared grimly at the ground. "I don't know," he said. "It was only about six months ago I first realized. Until then I just looked forward to seeing her, from one lunchtime to the next. I noticed she was growing into a beautiful girl, certainly, and enjoyed looking at her—but there was nothing improper in it. You know what I'm like, always at work. I never thought about women and things like that, I didn't have the time…"

"Well? And six months ago?"

The young farmer gave him an angry look, again a flush suffused his yellow skin. "Why do you ask? If you ask, I have to answer, and you're her father… . All right, then. In the spring there was a maid working for me, that Xenia from Horodenka, you remember, the one with the black hair? Well, I soon noticed she was slow at her work and trying to get round me by.... You won't get anywhere that way with me, woman, I thought. I've managed without your kind so far, and I'll continue to do so in the future.... But one evening…you see, Leibko, she was crafty the way she went about it. But the next morning I thought to myself, once doesn't count, a horse has four legs and even it sometimes stumbles. I wasn't at all ashamed of myself, you see. But when I set off to your place for lunch, I did suddenly begin to feel ashamed. I was embarrassed at the idea of Miriam seeing me and when I came into the inn I—I was dreadfully ashamed, and I couldn't help it, but from that moment on I looked at her differently from before. I thought it would sort itself out if I sent Xenia away, which I did that very day, but—" he gave a deep sigh "—it hasn't sorted itself out…"

There was an embarrassed blush on the Jew's weather-beaten features as well. A peasant, what do you expect, he thought, half indignantly, half with a feeling of superiority. "But since then?" he asked. "You must have said to yourself, Miriam's Jewish and a good girl, and Leibko's always been good to me, I must put the idea out of my head. Well, didn't you?"

"No," said Janko. "I didn't think anything except, I wish it were lunchtime already and I could go and see her. What was I expected to think?" he said angrily. "Only sixteen—and anyway, it's not the kind of thing where you think at all."

And he thinks he's a human being, was the the old man's reaction, but out loud he said, "But now that I'm asking you? Would you like to marry her?"

A look of immense astonishment appeared on the Ruthene's

face and stayed there, fixed. "But—but—that's—that's impossible," he said, stuttering. "She's a…"

"A Jew," said Leib Weihnachtskuchen with a smile. "But you could become a Jew."

"Me…me?!" The farmer's fists had automatically clenched. "If someone suggested that seriously…"

The Jew completed the sentence for him. "You'd knock him down. But there's another way out. If she were to become a Christian…"

Janko shook his head. "You wouldn't stand for that, Chane and you. Though…your wife's not very well, won't live for long, and you might come round if you felt really threatened."

"There's no hope of that," replied little Leib, in even more gentle tones than before. "As for my wife, God can do much. God can see to it that she's still looking out of the window when they carry your coffin past. And me? What could you threaten me with? Death? If I burden myself with such a sin I will lose the eternal delights of the world to come. Should I prefer a few years down here, years of the kind of life I have? So nothing doing there, my dear Janko. And now think: you can't marry her, but you don't want anyone else to. What's to become of her?"

Janko just sat there, head bowed, and did not reply.

"Well?" Leib insisted. "What's to become of her?"

"I don't know," the young man cried out. "You're right, it's horrid of me, stupid…but I won't stand for it. It'll lead to disaster, Leibko. A disaster, do you hear?"

"Just like there was on the *vygoda* all those years ago," Leib asked, "only a bit worse? Why not? You're stronger than me. Stronger than her, too. But until that happens, I'll put my trust in you. I think better of you than you do yourself."

The farmer buried his head in his hands. "Leibko," he cried, a sob in his voice, "if you only knew…"

"I know," the little Jew replied, "that you are a human being, not a brute beast. And that's sufficient for me. Goodbye, Janko."

3

With that, Leib strode off, head held high, and did not look round when Janko called out after him. And he retained his upright posture long after the Ruthene could no longer see him. He was not pretending to be stronger than he was, the sense of moral superiority was pulsing powerfully through his feeble frame.

But eventually his head sank onto his chest and his legs started to wobble so much he had to sit down by the roadside once more. It was the thought of the "animal" that was making him tremble and the disgust he felt was almost as strong as his dread. Even if nothing happened, the idea of his child being exposed to the hot, rank breath of such lust was bad enough. And what damage might the animal not do in its rage? With every breath his fear grew at the unprecedented, incomprehensible, disturbing situation he was suddenly faced with. He could not even get properly angry at such ingratitude and it was in vain that he tried to compose himself, to pray. He could trust in Him, and in his Miriam, but he could not gather his own thoughts. "I won't stand for it!…It'll lead to disaster"—he could not get the dull, hoarse sound of Janko's words out of his head.

"Mendele Shadchen!" he suddenly exclaimed, and it was as if a weight had been lifted from his breast. That was the answer! It had to be done quickly, immediately. And he dashed off to Halicz and through the wretched alleyways of the little town as though Janko were pursuing him brandishing a club. At last he reached the house with the shining brass plate:

> MENDELE PULVERBLITZ
> Beauro for Cattle, Hale, People and Fire
> German and Polish Advise
> Leters Wrote Legul Dockuments

Mendele's two official activities were acting as agent for various insurance companies and giving legal advice. The third and most lucrative, the one his fellow Jews used as his name: *shadchen*, marriage broker, he didn't even need to put on the plate. He had more than enough business as it was.

That was something Leib was about to discover. When he entered the first room, a kind of waiting room, Mendele's fat wife—she ran the "beauro" and was sitting behind a massive desk writing—scrutinized him with an arrogant stare and appeared to ignore his softly spoken, humble request to see her husband. Eventually, however, she asked him, "What for?"

"For my Miriam."

"Aha? I'm afraid you've had a wasted journey. My poor husband wouldn't be able to propose the kind of prince you would expect for your dowry. However, if you still want to talk to him, you must come back tomorrow." And indeed, Mendele obviously had visitors; from the adjoining room came the sound of several voices all shouting at each other at once. "He won't be finished before evening," she went on. "An engagement's being arranged in there."

It was a good thing she had told him, otherwise Leib would

have thought it was a divorce. A shrill female voice cried angrily, "The shame will send me to my grave! I won't agree unless you put down another five hundred crowns."

To this a vulgar male voice replied, "Not one heller. Because your Ruben's such a fine boy?! But if you promise to go to your grave before the wedding, I'll willingly add another hundred crowns."

"What are you waiting for?" Mendele's fat wife asked sharply when she saw Leib prick up his ears. He had recognized the woman's voice at once, it was a tailor's widow generally considered a disreputable character. Her son Ruben, a carter, was said to be coarse and dissolute. What kind of girl could it be where a woman like that could demand "another five hundred crowns"?

"I'll call back again later today," Leib said as he slipped out of the door.

"Next week'll be soon enough for us," the woman shouted after him. He pretended not to hear, although it cut him to the quick, that day of all days, when all his hopes were focused on that room. Otherwise it would not have troubled him. The woman had a reputation for being sharp-tongued and haughty, and then— Leib Weihnachtskuchen had come not to expect much in the way of kind words anyway.

Morosely he plodded along the bank of the Dniester, wondering if it wouldn't be best to go home after all. Then he remembered he had another piece of business to transact, one which would bring him thirty kreutzers. That is what Onufrij, the blacksmith, had said he would pay him, if he could get him twenty crowns for one of the two bills of exchange he had given him. Both were payable at three months, but one was for twenty-five crowns, the other for thirty—that is, a hundred or two hundred per cent per annum, whichever Leib could get. Onufrij himself didn't care which. Three months! No Podolian village blacksmith thinks that far ahead.

But Leib did, his honour as a loan-broker demanded it. "Of course," he said, talking to himself as was his habit, "I must ask both of them, Pan Kastanasiewicz and my Mosche,"—that referred to Moses Erdkugel to whom he owed money himself— "and whoever does it cheaper will get the business." And whom Leib asked first was not without importance for Onufrij's business. Since he felt no tie to the Armenian, as he did to Erdkugel, Leib headed for the estate office first of all.

Stefan Kastanasiewicz, the tenant of the Halicz estate, was in the yard, haggling with a farmer over an ox. He was an old man, thickset, with coarse, dull features that looked as if they had been hewn with an axe; the only prominent one was his hooked Armenian nose. He was wearing a threadbare smock with a hood that had once been black, but was now grey, and a greasy cap on his bushy white hair. To see him, alternately bawling and wheedling at the farmer, now and then expertly feeling the ox all over to swear in a whining voice that he couldn't add even ten kreutzers to the price, one would certainly have assumed he was a butcher. He had been, and before that a swineherd and drover, but that was forty years ago. Now he was a millionaire and part-owner of the estate; that he would soon be sole owner was a foregone conclusion. He had had his daughter educated at a seminary for young ladies in Cracow and bought himself an impoverished Polish count as son-in-law. His own son had also become Polish and was studying in Lemberg before he took over the estate. The old man stayed the way he had always been.

"Back again, dogshit?" he barked at the Jew. "With another of your extortionate loans? How often have I told you to stop pestering me with them or I'll set the dogs on you."

Leib did not turn a hair. "When you've finished, Pan Kastanasiewicz," he said.

Kastanasiewicz did not whistle for his dogs, not even after he had concluded his business with the farmer. He went into his office, leaving the door ajar. The Jew followed him.

"Well?" he asked. "What piece of knavery are you trying to inveigle me into today?"

Leib took out the bill of exchange for twenty-five crowns and explained the matter.

The Armenian flew into a rage. "You have the effrontery to come to me with that, you cut-throat? I'm expected to risk twenty crowns for a measly five? Onufrij's up to his ears in debt already. And permanently drunk. Anyway, when he was here not long ago he told me he always gives you two drafts. Where's the other one?"

"In my pocket," Leib replied. "And that's where it's staying. Mosche will do it for this one."

Kastanasiewicz cleared his throat. "Leibko," he said softly, almost pleadingly, "be reasonable. The other draft will be for thirty crowns, won't it? Look, I'll give you twenty for it, for you to give to Onufrij, and one crown for yourself. Since we're old friends, Leibko."

The little Jew shook his head. "That wouldn't be honest of me, Pan Kastanasiewicz."

Kastanasiewicz shot to his feet. "You scoundrel!" he roared. "What do I always say? An honest man should never let himself get involved with these swindling Jewish rogues." But then his anger was gone as quickly as it had come. "All right, this draft then. But for seventeen crowns."

"I'm sorry," said Leib, putting his hand on the doorknob.

"Eighteen."

"Let's hope we can do business another time," said Leib, and left. He'll send one of his men to fetch me back before I've got to Mosche's, he thought.

He was wrong in that, but only insofar as he had already reached the door to Mosche's house before the labourer from the estate caught up with him. And he could not turn back, because Moses was at the window. "Later, perhaps," he whispered to the labourer, and went in.

Moses Erdkugel, a man in his forties, did not live up to the name the would-be witty officials had given his family. He was not in the least globe-like, everything about him was angular, his figure, his pale face, even his nose was like a sharp mountain ridge. His expression was always earnest, but calm; no one had ever seen him angry or even irritated.

"Good evening, Reb Leib," was his measured reply to the other's greeting. "Good that you've come to see me, I was going to send for you. What have you got for me?"

Leib explained.

Erdkugel shook his head. "I'll leave that for the Armenian," he said equably. "He'll do it, I saw his labourer. You knocked on his door first and not on mine, so I'm happy to let him take precedence. I'd do that even if you offered me the other draft I'm sure Onufrij gave you just in case, and you won't want to do that, will you…. Now, let's talk about our business."

He sat down. "Fourteen years ago," he went on in the same

detached voice, "I lent you a hundred crowns to purchase your stock and furnishings. Paterski was willing to loan you the money, but he wanted fifty crowns interest every quarter; Kastanasiewicz was willing too, he demanded half that. I did it for forty crowns annually. Do you think you could have got the money cheaper anywhere else? Have you any complaints?"

"No!" Leib exclaimed.

"So we're agreed on that." His voice was as calm as ever, but his face seemed to become more and more angular; his hand, too, moved in short, sharp zigzags. "Why did I do it? Out of charity? That's what the Pole or the Armenian would have you believe. Not me. I never lie. I'm not a charity, I'm a businessman. Or out of fear of God?" A dark, apprehensive look came into his eyes. "If I have deserved His punishment, as the devout Jews claim, then He will not pardon me for one charitable deed. Or so that you will speak well of me to others? In that case I would have been a fool. Even then I knew I was despised and shunned by both Christians and our own people, and would ever remain so. Paterski and the Armenian do exactly the same as me, but they're respectable gentlemen, sit in the front row of the pews in church and the officials go to dine in their houses, for they are Christians. But I'm a Jew, so I had to go to prison, my seat in the synagogue is the last in the back row and I had to go a hundred and fifty miles from here to find a son-in-law.... So, why did I treat you like that all those years ago, Reb Leib?"

"So that I would bring you business," replied the little Jew. His heart was pounding with trepidation. This taciturn man had never spoken at such length to him before. It was a bad sign. Was yet another blow coming his way? "And I've done everything I possibly could..."

"That's a lie." The tone of voice, as unruffled as ever, seemed to contradict the sense. "You've always done the same as you did today. If I'm cheaper, I get the business, if I'm the same as the others, it's just a matter of chance. But I've put up with it. Why? I could lie about that, too, but I'll tell you the truth. Out of fear of our own people. None of them does anything about your poverty, they're all happy to make jokes about you, but if I had put the screws on you, they'd have all cried out, 'That usurer—a disgrace to the community—down with him!' But now—" he raised his hand "—but now let them cry as much as they like, I'm not going to lose my capital. We have always renewed your loan on the first of October, that means it's due in ten days time. I'm not going to renew it, I'm going to call it in."

"God of my fathers!" Leib gasped in horror. "But why?"

"At Christmas, Paterski's going to cancel your lease from the first of July. You'll be a pauper and won't be able to pay either capital or interest. And by now your stock and furnishings aren't worth half of what you owe me. I'm salvaging what I can."

Leib wrung his hands in despair. "Paterski won't do it. He keeps threatening to and never does. He won't get that rent from anyone else. I beg you…I beg you."

Moses stood up. "Our business is finished."

The little Jew swayed. He had to hold onto the chair to stop himself falling. "Have mercy," he cried. "At least wait until New Year to see if he does do it."

Moses had gone to the window, through which the red of the setting sun was pouring in. "I can't wait," he said, without looking round.

Leib shuffled up to him and humbly tugged at his coat.

"Mercy," he said, almost sobbing. "I'll do as much as I can for you in the three months."

The moneylender turned round slowly. "That's another lie," he said coldly. "Or is it? What can you do to prove you really mean it this time? Onufrij gave you two drafts, didn't he?"

Leib staggered back. He stood there for a minute, breathing heavily. Already his trembling hand was feeling its way towards his wallet when he was blinded by the red light of the setting sun. What could he say to Him after that?

His hand dropped. Silently he crept to the door. Then he dashed out of the house and along the street to the estate, breathless, as if Satan were at his heels. Only when he had reached the Armenian's door did he stop and try to compose himself before he entered.

"Out you go, dogshit!" Kastanasiewicz roared at him when he opened the door. "You get nowhere with Mosche, so you come to me? Out!"

Normally Leib would have ignored such a welcome, it was just the usual prelude to their business dealings. Now however, in his bemused state, he started and made to leave.

"Stop," the Armenian shouted. "Is the world going mad that even the Jews are touchy? I just wanted to say that it wasn't very nice of you, but that doesn't mean we can't do business together. Now: the draft for thirty crowns and one crown for you. Or one and a half, do you hear, one and a half crowns! Still not willing, you Jewish rogue?...Right, just to show you what a Christian's made of, we'll share. Two crowns fifty kreutzers."

But when he got nowhere with that, he took the lesser draft and paid out the twenty crowns.

Thank God! thought Leib when he was back in the street, at

least that's thirty kreutzers earned. And as for Mosche—if He did not allow me to do it, He will find something for me.

Still deeply depressed, but no longer crushed, he set off for the "beauro". As he approached, several people came out. Leib had guessed correctly. It was the tailor's widow and her son Ruben. The other two were an elderly couple he did not know. They must be village Jews, the man was wearing a fur hat, the woman a peasant headscarf. The two sides continued their argument out in the street, then parted without a farewell.

Oi weh, thought Leib, Mendele doesn't seem to have been able to do the deal, that means he'll be in a bad mood. When he entered, Mendele's wife called out to him, "Thank God you've brought your business today, otherwise I wouldn't have been able to sleep for worry." Mendele, however, beaming all over his face, gave him a friendly welcome.

Mendele Pulverblitz was still young, scarcely thirty, but he had taken over his father's business early and was now considered the best matchmaker in the area. His broad, cheerful red face inspired confidence, his patience and fluent tongue were inexhaustible; he seemed designed by Nature for his profession. Perhaps in creating Mendele Nature was compensating for the creation of Moses Erdkugel. If the latter consisted of nothing but sharp angles, the former was all curves, not simply his face and figure, his bright little eyes, his bulbous nose and his chin were also round, even his short, thick lips which, as he was eating bilberries just at the moment, stuck out of his face like the fruit of the deadly nightshade.

"Sit down, Reb Leib, sit down," he said in a friendly voice, without stopping eating. "I need to wet my whistle first, all the talking I've had to do.... Right then, my wife's already told me why you're here. How old is the girl?...Sixteen already?! A bit late, isn't it, why've you put it off so long? But why am I asking, I know the answer. You've been sitting out there waiting to see if God will let a little piece of dowry drop from heaven. God doesn't do that very often, Reb Leib, we have to earn it ourselves. Not that I'm criticising you, I know you work your fingers to the bone." The words flowed unstoppably from Mendele's lips, which grew blacker and blacker the more the bowl with the berries emptied.

"It'll be difficult—you know that already.... But don't worry, I'll find something. If anyone can do it, I can. Any fool can make straightforward matches; I like a challenge. The engagement that was signed and sealed here today—" he thumped the table with his fist "—there's no one in the whole of Poland could have arranged that but Mendele Shadchen. You can rely on me. But—what's in it for me?"

Leib came out of his trance with a start. "That depends...that depends on the bridegroom you find."

Mendele burst out laughing. "Of course! Depending on whether I bring you a Jewish prince or just the son of Moses Montefiore!"—Every Jew in eastern Europe was familiar with the name of the English philanthropist. For them he was the embodiment of wealth and fame.—"Nonsense," Mendele went on in an acid voice, "are you going to give me ten crowns or are you not?"

"Reb Mendele—" the little Jew was about to start on a longish speech, but he was interrupted.

"Yes or no?" The matchmaker had stood up. He could be brief when it suited him.

Once more Leib gave a start. "Yes," he sighed, almost inaudibly.

"Fine. That's agreed, then. To be paid on the engagement. And now, the dowry?"

Again the little innkeeper sighed and shyly started on a long-winded explanation of their plan to take their future son-in-law into their house for a few years.

Mendele cut him off. "Nonsense! From what I hear, you're going to be thrown out yourselves. Even if not, who'd want to starve with you? Mendele Shadchen is not acquainted with the kind of riffraff who'd agree to that. If that was the only way, I'd have sent you off the moment you came. But I know your daughter, I know that she's a big, heavy girl, and healthy, thank God, and that gives me hope there might be something better. We must find a man who will demand nothing of you, one who'll even pay for the trousseau himself."

Leib began to feel apprehensive. "But it must be a good man," he said hesitantly, "and healthy...and not too old..."

"Of course! There's one comes to mind right away. Seventeen years old, constitution of an ox, and that he's never told a lie in his life I can swear on my mother's grave.... The son of Reb Srulze. Dubs is their German name."

"Him!" Leib exclaimed, horrified. "The boy's a deaf mute, a simpleton."

"Not at all. If you knew how clever he is. The answers he gives."

"But he can't speak."

"I mean with his hands. And he's after the girls already, as if he were thirty, not seventeen.... But if he's too stupid for you, I know a cleverer one. He can even read and write German, well enough to put the whole Jewish community in the shade. A widower with two children, to be sure, but he's only thirty and makes a good living with his legal advice..."

"You don't mean Avrumele Sturm?"

"Who else? For a few years he called himself Albert Sturm, but now he's an honest Avrumele again and intends to stay that way. What are you staring at me like that for? Because he spent a few months...? All because of a misunderstanding?"

"It was three years and it was serious fraud. It was the shame that sent his poor wife to an early grave."

"But that would be nothing to do with your daughter. And Avrumele swears the public prosecutor misunderstood the matter because he's not a businessman. Can that be true, does the public prosecutor have to be a businessman as well?!—But if you insist, I've got a third one for you. And with him you won't say anything, nothing at all apart from, Reb Mendele, I thank you... . You understand?"

"Tell me," Leib asked.

Mendele stood up, a solemn expression had come over his face and Leib, tense with apprehension, followed suit.

"Sit down," said Mendele. "You're a weak man and the joy might be too much for you." Then he pointed out into the twilight beyond the open window. "Him."

Leib looked in the direction he was pointing. Outside, the mighty waters of the Dniester were flowing down from the Carpathians to the plains. From across the river the lights of a large building, its outline fading into the dark, shone out...

"The sawmill?!" he gasped. "Reb David Münzer's Nathan?...That would be...a blessing. A true blessing." His voice failed.

"You see?!" said Mendele triumphantly. "And what will you say when you hear that the blessing is even greater than you think? It's not the son, it's the father himself. Reb David Münzer!" He emphasized the syllables separately, savouring each one, as if it were a tasty morsel.

Leib drew back in horror. "The old man?...Impossible."

Mendele whipped round. "Whaaat?!" he cried, drawing out the word and putting his hand behind his ear as if he couldn't believe he had heard right. "Are you out of...?" He seemed to be struck dumb with astonishment.

"But just think," said Leib shyly, "he must be perhaps sixty years older than my Miriam..."

"A hundred!" the matchmaker cried, throwing his arms in the air. "Did you hear, Beile?" he said, turning to his wife. (Beile was a corruption of Bella.) "Leib the village innkeeper says no when I offer him Reb David Münzer for his daughter. A good thing I have a witness, otherwise no one would believe me!"

"Serves you right," came the response from the kitchen. "Throw him out."

Pulverblitz nodded. "If that's not acceptable," he said, turning to face the little man, suddenly cold and calm, "then go, and don't come back again. I'm not interested in dealing with madmen. You know who you are, but who is Reb David? The richest man in Halicz, devout, respected, hardworking—and you won't find another steam sawmill like that in the whole of Poland. Goodbye, Reb Leib."

Leib just stood there, bewildered, the thoughts going round and round in his head. David Münzer really was everything Mendele had said, and still pretty sprightly for his age. But he was at least seventy and had recently been widowed for the third time.

There were still five of his children living at home. In his mind he saw the wrinkled face of the old man, his eyes looking wearily out from under heavy, reddened lids, his bent figure. He shut his eyes. He shuddered at the thought of handing over a girl in the flower of youth and beauty to those withered arms. But then the words his wife had said came back to him, Janko's hoarse voice.... He twisted and turned his hat in his hands, unable to make up his mind

"Reb David won't get any younger, however long you wait," Pulverblitz mocked. "Now go."

"Forgive me." Leib tried to pull himself together. "Even a poor father hopes his child..." Mendele made an impatient gesture and Leib did not dare complete the sentence. "I won't come to a decision today," he said, "Chane must have her say... . Reb David...I wouldn't have thought he would have wanted to get married again."

"Because you're so clever! All the others have thought of it. His house is besieged. And the brides he's offered! I'm negotiating for his Nathan about a girl from Husiyatin. She has a dowry of twenty thousand crowns, her uncle's a miracle-working rabbi. But it's not settled yet. And why? Because the family would prefer the father! Word of honour! And why not? Could a woman wish for better? And what's seventy when you're the way he is? Compared with him I'm an old man. But Reb David? 'No,' he says. 'The Husiyatin girl's too light for me, and what do I need more money for? If I should decide to get married again, it must be a lovely, plump, heavy girl.' That's why I thought of your daughter. But instead of weeping for joy—but let's not go into that again. And he'd probably have thrown me out anyway, there'd be reason enough."

"What reason?" Leib asked, hurt.

"Think of your lease. He'd be marrying you and your wife along with the girl. And even if not, can't a man like him expect money as well, even if she is a plump, heavy girl? And are you from a religious family?"

"Yes I am," Leib replied eagerly. "My great-grandfather was a rabbi's assistant."

Pulverblitz gave a scornful laugh. "And your grandfather? Your father? You? Have you ever studied Talmud? A peasant can sell schnapps to peasants. But what's the point of all this? It was a stupid idea. 'What?' he'll say, 'Leib's daughter? A village girl?'"

"There's no shame in that," said Leib.

"No shame, but no gain, either. Can she run a big household? Bring up the children? Has she learnt how to converse with people from your peasants? Without mentioning that out in the villages things sometimes happen…"

"What?!" Leib exclaimed, horrified and therefore rather loud.

"Don't shout like that. I'm not suggesting your daughter's done anything wrong. But sometimes things do happen, very rarely, thank God, but even if it's only once in a hundred years, it's something that has to be borne in mind."

"What?" Leib repeated hoarsely. He felt as if the room had suddenly started spinning round and the chubby matchmaker with it. Mendele assumed it was an exclamation of outrage and went on in placatory tones, "As I said, something like that ought not to happen with a Jewish girl, and God forbid I should think it of your daughter, but the engagement I've just arranged…. Do you know the people? The father of the bride is a rich timber merchant from Sniatyn, he was given the contract for the sleepers for the new line from Lemberg to Czernowitz. So last autumn he moved to a village close to his forest to supervise the work himself. And now? Now he has to lay out a thousand crowns to buy Ruben, the carter, as his son-in-law so that his eldest daughter has a husband to go with her child. Just imagine, she had an affair with a forester. And the father's fortunate that Reb David Münzer is a partner in the contract—next spring the line will be built here, as you know. So he comes here and Reb David recommends him to me. No *shadchen* in the whole of Poland could do anything for him. I did, of course. What can I not do? I don't like praising myself, but I have to say…"

What now followed was, despite Mendele's aversion to self-praise, an exhaustive account of what he had to say about himself, and that was good for poor Leib Weihnachtskuchen. It gave him time to get over his alarm, so that the matchmaker did not notice it at all. But thinking clearly, coming to a decision, was still impossible. After a brief farewell, he dashed off.

He only stopped, to try and gather his thoughts, when he had left the little market town behind him and was alone on the solitary, moonlit road to Vinkovce. But he found it impossible, the blood was still pounding too furiously in his head.

"God in heaven!" he suddenly exclaimed, raising his arms to the sky.

It was a cry of profound dismay, and the horror at what he had just heard was as much part of it as the fear of the danger threatening him. The thought of the danger had come to him earlier, of course, but then he had dismissed it as madness and begged God and his daughter for forgiveness. A Christian and a Jew—to his mind it was against nature, like a union of wolf and lamb; it never happened, it never could happen, so he did not need to tremble at the idea. All he was afraid of was that Janko might resort to violence, but a love affair—no. Not just because his Miriam was a good, obedient girl, but because she was a Jewish girl. And now it had happened, in this very land, in this very year. He felt as if the ground were swaying under his feet. Mendele was right. Even if it only happened once in a hundred years, it had to be taken into account—and Mendele knew nothing of Janko.

"O God in heaven!" The words came from his lips again but this time softly, almost inaudible, even to Leib himself, a prayer from the depths of his soul. "You can do anything.... You will see that all this turns out for the best.... You will, won't you?"

His lips moved, but no sound came as he prayed a silent prayer. He stood there, on the dusty road, looking up to the heavens so that his face was bathed in the moonlight. He felt as if He must send him a sign...but there was no movement apart from the gentle soughing of the wind as it ruffled the bushes. And yet, the longer he stood there looking, all around him silence and light, light and silence, the more the weight gradually lifted from his heart. Above were the moon and stars in their eternal courses, around him the fields of stubble and the dust of the road shimmered like pure silver. It was no different from what he had seen a thousand times before, but that night it was balm to his soul and his poor heart beat more calmly again.

Strangely comforted, he continued on his way. It must be late, he thought, probably about ten, his wife and daughter would be worried. He tried to stride out at a fast pace, but it was impossible, his poor, weak, bandy legs could only manage to drag themselves slowly through the deep dust. He grew wearier and wearier until he could go on no longer. When he reached the bench by the well, where he had sat with Janko that afternoon, he automatically hobbled across to it. Usually he would have avoided the bench—it was late and the figure of the crucified Christ shone bright and clear—but now he sat down on it without further ado. "Just for a few minutes," he muttered to himself as his head sank back against the upright of the cross. Then he heard the clock of the church in Halicz strike, a dull, distant sound as if from many miles away. He counted two strokes. "Half past," he muttered sleepily. "Half past nine or already half past ten?" Then the veil over his eyes thickened and he was asleep.

When he woke again with a start, he was confused and did not know where he was, though he did know what had woken him. It was Miriam's voice, a worried voice calling out for him. Then he heard it again, nearer this time, if still far enough away. "Father! Father!" It sounded frightened, like a cry for help. Trembling, he sat up and rubbed his eyes. He was awake and he knew how he came to be there, and yet he must still be dreaming. What was his daughter doing, out at night, on the country road? And now he could hear a distant step and then her voice again. But not calling out for him, she was singing. With each step she took the words came to him more clearly:

> Janko, don't come here again,
> Father's warned me about men,
> Mother's always nagging too,
> Telling me the things they do.
>
> Let her scold me, let him moan,
> Told is not the same as done.
> I must find out for myself—
> Janko, meet me at the well.

"Miriam!" Leib shouted, horrified, and dashed towards her.

"Father!" With a cry of joy she threw her arms around him. "Where have you been all this time? We were so frightened. I suppose you fell asleep by the roadside here? Poor father."

He freed himself from her embrace. "Miriam," he cried, scrutinizing her glowing features in an agony of fear, "what was that you were singing?"

Presumably she did not hear the question. "Fallen asleep?!" she repeated, laughing. "It was a good thing Mother sent me to look for you, then. True, she did say, 'Only as far as the woods, not one step further,' but I said to myself, 'What can happen to me?' and kept going. But come along, come along, Mother's getting anxious. She couldn't stop wailing, 'I'm sure something's happened to him'."

He let her put her arm round him and urge him forward. But then he asked again, "Why were you singing that song?"

"What song?" she asked in astonishment. "I can't remember what the last one was. On the way I sang all the songs I know, calling out for you in between. I was rather frightened, I have to admit, worried about you and then all alone in the dark...I felt a bit better when I could hear the sound of my own voice."

He breathed a sigh of relief and was able to trot along more quickly beside her. But then he stopped again and said, "Miriam, you've never lied to me, have you? You're telling me the truth now, aren't you? You were just singing because you were afraid?"

She looked at him in bewilderment. "Yes, of course. Why else? Are you angry with me about it? I thought that was only Mother. She says it's not proper because I'm grown up now. But really old women in the village sing those songs."

"Christian women!" he said. "But you're a Jewish girl. You

won't sing those songs any more, will you? And you'll always stay my little Miriam, my good girl?"

"Of course," she laughed. "But now we must get on."

"No," he said, and his voice was quivering with emotion, quite solemn, "not like that." He stopped and placed his hand on her head. "You are all I have in the world. You must promise me properly."

She became serious too, she had never seen him like this before. Was it the moonlight that gave his eyes that moist gleam? "I promise," she said. "I will always obey your wishes."

After that he did not say another word until they reached the inn. She was silent too. Though she could scarcely say why, she had had a funny feeling, back there on the road.

Outside the house Chane came to meet them, sobbing. "You were afraid to come home," she cried. "What news do you bring?" He tried to calm her down, but when she pressed him to tell her what had happened, he turned her away with a brusque, "Tomorrow," adding, "I've had enough for today."

"Enough…enough…" was the word that kept going through his mind until he sank, exhausted, onto his bed.

4

Sleep took pity on him. After just a few minutes, during which all the experiences of the day—a day like none he had been through before—swirled round his mind in a wild, tormenting reel, he was oblivious to himself and all his troubles.

It was only towards morning that they came to him in a dream. He saw himself in a large, festive room, which he had never seen before; it must be in David Münzer's house, for he was sitting at the head of the table, Miriam beside him, deathly pale and woebegone. "I didn't sing again, father," she whispered, and he could understand what she said, even though he was a long way away from her and the many wedding guests were making a noise and shouting. But then all at once they disappeared, just the bridal couple were left, sitting in their places of honour, and he was still in his corner. Suddenly Janko burst in, brandishing an axe and rushing towards Miriam. Leib cried out and tried to thrust himself between them but his limbs refused to obey. "Mercy," he groaned and raised his arm. "Janko—" A cold hand was placed on his brow and he woke.

It was his wife's hand. She had woken him because he had emitted such a terror-stricken moan. He looked around—the first grey light of morning was trickling in through the little windows of the bedroom—and gave Chane a distraught stare. He felt he had never seen her face so pale, so emaciated. "Are you ill?" he stammered.

"No more than usual," she replied in acid tones. "But what's the matter with you? What happened between you and Janko yesterday to make you dream of him?"

"Nothing...later...after prayers."

He got up, performed the usual ablutions, put on the *tefillin* and turned his face towards the east. This was always the high point of his day, but never before had he found such comfort, such significance in the familiar, cherished words: "Praise be unto Thee, Eternal One, our God, that raiseth up all that be bowed down," and then, "that directeth the steps of men." How they soothed his poor, trembling soul. He had always directed his steps according to His commandment, yesterday too, he could still look Him in the eye. A man who could say that did not need to tremble...

His features were still suffused with a faint glow from this trusting faith when, after their meagre breakfast, his wife commanded, "Tell me." He did not intend to keep anything from her but, despite his mood of exaltation, he began with the part of yesterday's experiences which would bring him the fewest reproaches: his interview with Mendele Shadchen.

She listened, unmoving except that from time to time a quiver would run through her wasted frame and the lines round her mouth become even sharper. When, for example, he told her about the deaf mute and then Avrumele Sturm. Only when he mentioned the name of the elderly suitor did she start; her hand clutched his arm in a feverish grip. "Reb David Münzer...and what did you say?"

"That…that I would discuss it with you."

"Thank God!" Two patches of an unhealthy red appeared on her withered cheeks. "It would have been just like you to reject such a piece of good fortune."

"Good fortune?" he said timidly. "You think…"

"That we should prostrate ourselves in the dust and thank God if something comes of it," she replied. "Yes, that's what I think. Don't say anything," she went on harshly, as he was about to speak. "What you're going to say I've said to myself a thousand times already. Years ago it kept me awake at nights, and now, since she's grown up—I'm not blind and I'm not stupid, I foresaw how we would be able to provide for her…. Provide! God help us!" She began to sob. "I pleaded with God. 'Work a miracle,' I said, 'she's such a good, beautiful girl.'" Two tears suddenly rolled down her cheeks; she hastily wiped them away. "But miracles don't happen any more. That's probably the best of what's possible." She shivered and pulled her thin shawl closer round her shoulders. "I had prepared myself for worse," she said dully. "A decent, rich husband, and his age is a comfort, after all…"

"Chane!" he exclaimed in horror at what she was implying.

"Am I saying I hope he dies? But a husband of seventy, a wife of sixteen…" Then she asked anxiously, "Do you think Mendele was serious about trying?"

He went through the interview with Mendele again, and this time he told her the end of the discussion.

"Nonsense," she said scornfully. "Mendele just made that up to give you a fright. And if there really is a Jewish girl like that—you hear of calves with five legs—what's it to do with us?…So it looks as if Mendele is genuinely willing to try. He's clever and never attempts the impossible, so perhaps he'll succeed." She heaved a sigh of relief. "We'll go and see him tomorrow to discuss the details."

"That soon?!" The exclamation came out involuntarily.

"What do you want to wait for?" she asked bitterly. "For Reb David to get younger or for you to get rich? I haven't enough time left for that. I'm a sick woman. I'd like to die in peace, and I can only do that when I've seen my child underneath the *chuppah* with her bridegroom. Or do you want to wait until the summer so that Reb David can marry a homeless girl?"

Leib started. She still didn't know what Mosche had said to him, and it was only nine days until the beginning of October. Later, he told himself. Just think of the row she'll kick up, not that it will make any difference. But then he plucked up all his courage and hesitantly, falteringly, revealed their new plight.

She took it even worse than he had feared. A flood of laments and reproaches poured over his bowed head. "Oh well done," she said, "isn't that just the way to win people over! And you want to reject Reb David's proposal? What else is there can save us apart from him standing security for us?" He did not reply to that but it did not cause him too much concern. Reb David hasn't proposed anything yet, he thought to himself, and as for our debt to Mosche, is it my fault if he wanted me to do something He would not allow?

It was her final shot that filled him with dismay. "And why has all this happened to us? Because of that peasant! Now let us see your friend Janko save us!"

His consternation was so visible she noticed it despite her agitation. "Well?" she asked. "It seems to me you've tried that already. You were dreaming about it—you cried out, 'Janko, mercy!'—What was his reply?"

He shook his head. "No," he said tonelessly, "my dream was sparked off by something different. Janko couldn't help me...and since yesterday I'd bite off my own tongue rather than ask him. Since yesterday..." He had to struggle for breath. "You have to know everything." And he described what had happened by the cross, word for word; the only thing he could not bring himself to tell her was the awful suspicion he had entertained for a moment. She'd never forgive me that, he thought, and she'd be right.

The effect was different from what Leib had feared. True, the reproaches rained down on his head, making the timid man cower until only the top of his faded skullcap was visible above the table, but Chane clearly felt nothing of the fear Janko's passion had inspired in him. On the contrary, hands on hips ready for battle, she declared defiantly, "I'll see to him once and for all, this very day. Cry if you like, but that's one of your customers I'm going to get rid of for good. For good!"

"Cry?" The head with the faded skullcap ventured a little above the table. "I'll jump for joy, if you manage it. But..."

"What?" she asked sharply.

"I mean.... You didn't hear him ranting and raving yesterday. He seems to be out of his mind as far as Miriam's concerned. If he's provoked..."

"He'll murder us all?!" she said scornfully. "Oh yes, a fine friend you've found yourself there. But I'm not afraid. I know—how—how to deal—with animals—I—"

That was as far as she got. A convulsive fit of coughing threatened to choke her. Her hollow cheeks went red, her wasted body shook. Panic-stricken, Leib tried to help her, but she waved him away. Finally the fit was over and she sank back on the bench, exhausted.

"Off you go," she murmured. "Later."

Leib slipped out of the house in a gloomy mood. It was another beautiful day. Autumn is the only season that brings this seemingly Godforsaken heath country a succession of fine days. The sun in the clear blue sky had a summer warmth, but Leib shivered with a cold that seemed to chill him to the heart. Worry and care wherever he looked—and every hour brought new cares. The way Chane coughed, the way she looked! Not that it had just started today, no, but that was something else he had not really paid attention to as he dragged out his wretched existence from day to day.

He closed his eyes. My Lord and God, he thought, not that, at least spare us that.

Then he heard someone call his name. It was Onufrij, the smith, who had come for his money. "You did get it?" he asked.

Leib nodded. "And for the cheaper bill."

"You did? Really?" The well-fed man with the suspiciously red nose in his broad face said it offhandedly, as if the matter scarcely concerned him. "Hand it over, then."

They went into the inn and completed their business. And since he was there, Onufrij got Leib to bring him a bottle of schnapps, despite the early hour.

"I'm only sorry," he said after he had downed the first glass in one gulp, "that I didn't go for forty crowns."

"Why?" Leib asked. "Do you need that much?"

"Oh you stupid Yid!" The smith laughed a contented laugh. "You can never have too much money. And now I've no worries about being able to pay it back. You know—the railway…"

"Yes, they'll be building it here in the spring. But why do you expect to earn money from it, Pan Onufrij?"

The smith laughed out loud. "Oh you numskull! What's my trade, eh? And what's a railway, eh? You haven't seen one, but I have. When I was in Lemberg last spring. The iron horse's been running there from Cracow for several years now. And it runs on rails, iron rails, Leibko. Now you tell me who it is who forges the rails and nails them to the sleepers. The glazier, perhaps? There'll be thousands to be earned. A pile of crowns. That big!" He held his hand high above the table. "And they won't haggle about the price with a poor tradesman the way these stingy peasants do when they come to get their old nags shod. Who's building the railway? The Emperor, that's who. Now d'you understand, Leibko?"

The little Jew had hardly been paying attention, he was immersed in his own gloomy thoughts once more. "Of course," he said, "there's money to be made there."

"But not just from the rails," Onufrij went on. "Did you know that the emperor's officials are coming here in a few days time? Such fine gentlemen as you've never seen before! Every one has a large paunch and a gold cross on his chest as big as a window-frame. Given to them by the Emperor. And why are they coming, you ask? To mark out the route for the iron horse. And they won't take the ground for nothing. The Emperor will pay for every inch with gold. You understand?"

"But are you sure," Leib asked, "that the railway will be built on your fields?"

"Whaaat?!" This time the smith burst into such a braying laugh it gave the little Jew a start and Miriam peered round the door in curiosity. "Oh it's true what they say, isn't it? Of a thousand Jews there's only one stupid one, but his stupidity makes up for all the rest. Will the railway go over my ground? Hahaha! If I laugh any more it'll kill me. Over who else's. Over your Janko's, that miserable skinflint, God damn him. What pulls the carriages on the railway? An iron horse, as I've told you already. How it does it, I don't know, that is, I don't know how it can run on its own, no one does. People say there's something…fishy about it, that…" He looked round nervously and hurriedly crossed himself three times.

"The devil?" asked Miriam with a laugh. She was still standing in the doorway.

"Shh!" Again the smith looked round nervously. "But that's nonsense. Our Emperor wouldn't have…have dealings with…I'm more inclined to believe what other people say, namely that there's an evil spirit inside each of the iron horses, one of the damned, but the Lord God Himself locked them in, as a favour to our Emperor, and now they have to do the work. They don't like it, of course, and that's why there's such a fearful stench coming out, and smoke—I tell you…"

"But I still don't understand why—" said little Leib.

"The track's bound to go past my house? A child could see that. I don't know what's inside, no honest Christian does, but outside it's made of iron and every mile something'll go wrong with it, that I do know. Well then? If that happens here in Vinkovce, who else is going to repair it but me? Eh? And they're going to put it where it takes me half an hour to get there, are they? Eh?"

He held the bottle up to the light. It was almost empty. "Another bottle, Leibko. Yes, there are good times coming."

"God grant they do," said Leib with a sad smile and filled the bottle. Then he slipped out to see how his wife was.

He found her in the kitchen, preparing their scant meal. The smoke from the stove kept setting off her cough. "You should take things easy," he said. "Couldn't Miriam…just for this once…?"

"Why today?" she asked. "You're a strange man, Leib," she went on, her voice now calm, with just a hint of bitterness and sorrow. "You only realized yesterday that you had a grown-up daughter, and only today that you wife's dying."

"Dying!?" he exclaimed in horror. "God forbid!"

"Perhaps He'll have pity on me," she said, "and not take me until I've seen my child under the *chuppah*. But it mustn't take too long, otherwise…"

She fell silent, pressing her lips together. He too had to compose himself before he could say, "Chane, we have to go and see a doctor, right away."

She shook her head. "It's too late for a doctor to do anything for me," she said in a matter-of-fact voice, as if she were talking about something unconnected with her. "It's my chest. My mother—may she rest in peace—died of the same disease…and at about the same age, as it happens. I'll be forty next *purim*… . Perhaps I'm wrong," she said when she saw how devastated he looked, "but…"

She broke off. Once more the thin lips were pressed firmly together.

"My God," he sighed softly, "my God."

"We can always ask the doctor tomorrow," she said, though only to soothe him, "since we'll be in Halicz anyway. If my wishes were all that mattered, we'd go and see Mendele Shadchen today, but I don't think it would be a good idea to let him see how desperate we are."

He just nodded and was about to slip out again, but she held him back. "I suppose Onufrij's going to sit there all day," she asked, apparently unconcerned, "until they carry him home this evening?"

"Probably," he replied.

"Then I won't be able to talk to Janko today, and I don't know if I'll be able to do it tomorrow.... I don't want any disagreement between us," she added hesitantly, "and since you know more about it and are very much against it..."

"But how can you say that, Chane?" he said timidly. "I haven't said a word against it. If you think it's the right thing..."

He saw her lips twitch with impatience and stopped. Now he knew what this was about. It was what she always did when she regretted some decision she had come to. She was too stubborn to admit what she had wanted to do was wrong, so she used his insistence as a pretext to conceal her own change of mind.

In such cases Leib naturally considered it his duty to make it easy for her.

"Well, yes," he said, launching into his counter-argument to order and trying to sound as firm as he could, "actually I was against it. Why bother? He's a coarse peasant and you're a sick woman. You won't get him to see reason, either—"

Chane interrupted. "All right, there's no need to go on and on about it. I told you it's not going to happen. But then you mustn't talk to him about it either. If he does bring it up, you're to say: We'll discuss that when the time comes. At the moment we haven't found a husband for her, and since we're so poor we might never find one.—But if, with God's help, we do find one, then you definitely don't tell him that. Understood?"

"Not quite," he said hesitantly. "Chane," he went on in

pleading tones, as if he were confessing to an unforgivable sin, "you know I can't tell a lie...and anyway it wouldn't solve the problem. Miriam regards him as her friend, she's sure to tell him about the engagement right away—"

"She will not," Chane broke in, "if I forbid her to. I'll have to think up some excuse, of course, we can't tell her the truth. In her heart Miriam's still the child she was ten years ago, thank God, and she doesn't need to know why that ugly peasant comes here every day and what's going through his mind when he gawps at her. She mustn't even suspect it, which is why we mustn't make too much of it. And we have to keep him in ignorance, we'll even have to put up with him coming here every day. If we do ban him, she'll want to know the reason, or he'll lie in wait for her somewhere and frighten her with the horrible things he'll say. That's another reason why I've bowed to your will," she concluded. "So that's settled."

"Yes," he hurried to agree. Now he saw it too. For a moment the story Mendele had told him came back to mind, but he immediately said to himself again, God forgive me the sin against my child. And it wasn't just a sin, it was nonsense. Chane knew a lot more about these things than he did; if the merest shadow of such a danger were possible, she would foresee it. Of course she was right in this, as usual. If Janko thought there was no immediate likelihood of an engagement, he was so shy and timid he would not have the courage to speak to Miriam.

Though what he would do when he did hear of it... . The little man shuddered as last night's dream came back to him. It was almost as if he could see the axe gleaming as it came plunging down onto the head of his beloved daughter.

Chane gave him a sharp look. "Something else?" she asked

curtly. He told her about his dream. "Forgive me," he said as he finished, "but perhaps…perhaps God sent it as a warning…"

"He doesn't need dreams for that," she said. "He's given us minds of our own so we can avoid danger. We'll have to be on our guard, of course. It could be you think the man is more dangerous than he really is, or he might calm down with time, but if you're right, then Miriam must be out of the house when he hears of the engagement. Let him vent his rage in Halicz then. At worst, any misfortune he'll bring down will be on himself, not on us."

As always, he took heart from her resolution. There was only one thing in which he felt superior to her, in his understanding of what God wanted from men, in all worldly matters he deferred to her better judgment. And so he felt easier in his mind when he returned to the taproom, where Onufrij had already drunk half of the second bottle. That was nothing unusual for the Vinkovce blacksmith. He was nowhere near drunk, just a little merry.

"A crown an inch," he was muttering to himself, "two…three…four crowns." And when the Jew reappeared, "Twenty crowns, Leibko, you fool, twenty crowns an inch. Or thirty? What do you think?"

"Yes, yes," said Leib, sitting down behind the counter.

He could not chat to his customer, which he normally considered his duty, for the moment his heart was too heavy. The scene with Janko, which had caused him so much fear and trembling, wouldn't take place now, but he was still concerned about what would happen when they met again. He would just have to grin and bear that, however, but his wife, his poor wife…. His father had concluded the engagement without asking him and he'd seen her for the first time at the marriage ceremony. The difference in their characters had quickly become evident and he too, not just Chane, had suffered grievously under it. From very early on he had submitted to her in everything in which He did not demand greater obedience. Penury had been their lot from the beginning and in such an environment her physical charms had soon faded. And yet she was not just his lawful wedded spouse, the mother of his daughter, she was the wife of his bosom, of his love, just as much as any woman who had been freely chosen and was one with her husband in thought, word and deed. His wife was ill, was dying, and he had not noticed, had just thought, she's coughing, poor woman, but she's always has a cough, with God's help she'll get over it. But what could he have done, in any case, to look after her, to care for her, if he had noticed? But no, that was not an excuse. Even the poorest man could ask the doctor, even the weakest could earn a little more.

What a sinner I am, he thought, overcome with remorse, and then the words came bursting out: "Save her, God of mercy, I will do penance."

"What?" bawled the blacksmith, putting his hand behind his ear. "Louder. And I can't understand your damn' Jewish, either. Come here," he went on, "I've got something I want to tell you. Here, I say."

Leib got up and went timidly over towards the window where the smith was sitting. As he did so he idly glanced out…. He suddenly stared and his whole body started to tremble.

Heavens, what was that?! Striding down the village street towards the house came Janko. But it was not only the hour that was unusual—by the clock on the priest's house it was scarcely ten—but also his dress. He had put on the suit of clothes he had inherited from his father which he normally only wore on high days and holidays: the long jerkin of white-tanned ox-hide, lined with fur and held together by a black, silver-mounted belt, the high, brown sheepskin cap on his head and over his shoulder the axe with the richly carved wooden handle, the sign of a free farmer who ploughed his own land.

The axe!

Frozen with horror, the little Jew stared at the blade, gleaming in the sunshine, and could not move as it came closer and closer. It was only when the smith also noticed Janko approaching and exclaimed in astonishment, "Janko—and all dolled up?!" that he felt the blood in his veins thaw and was able to move again. He turned, to go into the kitchen and warn the women, but it was too late, the young peasant was already coming into the taproom.

When he saw Leib, he doffed his cap and greeted him formally: "In the name of Christ, His blessing be on this house." This too was unusual, but it was not that alone which drained the power of movement from Leib's limbs. He had lived in the village long enough to know precisely why Janko had come. The Sunday best on a weekday, the formal greeting—the young peasant had come to ask for Miriam's hand and was following the conventions usual among his people. Everything was as it should be, apart from the two witnesses the prospective bridegroom normally brought with him.

It was so obvious even Onufrij noticed. "What?" he said, roaring with laughter, "Janko's going to get himself a little wife?! Hohoho!"

Janko started. It was only now that he saw there was someone else in the room. His face, that had been flushed with agitation, paled, his shoulders slumped. He did not reply, but turned away and stared at the floor in embarrassment.

Still roaring with laughter, the smith went over to him. "I've always said our Janko's the most handsome lad in the village, hahaha," he mocked. "And dressed to kill as well! I once saw a monkey dancing in Lemberg. It wasn't anything like as beautifully dressed—though in looks I'd say it could compete with you."

"Shut up," said Janko, drawing back.

"Oho," cried the smith, rolling up his sleeves. "Is that the way for a young puppy like you to talk to his elders and betters? A skinflint everyone looks down on to a decent man everyone in the village respects because he knows how to live and let live?"

Janko took another step back. "Shut up," he repeated hoarsely.

"But why shouldn't I offer you my congratulations?" the other mocked. "Who's the lucky girl? Surely not..." He looked at Leib and broke out into uncontrollable laughter again.

The little Jew was still standing there, paralysed, unable to speak. Now that it looked as if the mockery was about to be turned on him, he grasped his throat, as if to pull off the invisible hands that were choking him. "Onufrij..." he stammered, but that was all he managed to say.

Then he heard his wife's voice in the adjoining room. "Miriam, you stay here," she said sharply. "There's two drunks arguing out there, that's nothing for you." She came into the taproom. "Janko?" she murmured. "What's going on here?"

"Hurray!" the smith bellowed when he saw her. "Here comes your prospective mother-in-law, you'll have the courage to speak now, won't you?"

Janko just stood there, deathly pale and panting, his chest rising and falling convulsively. "Swine!" he gasped hoarsely, brandishing his axe. "One more word and...'

Chane sped over to the window and flung it open. "Help!" she shouted out into the street. Leib too had found his voice again, and the strength to force himself between the two.

"No need for that," laughed the smith, pushing him aside with a flap of the hand that sent the feeble man staggering against the wall, "it's just a joke. But I would like to know who the lucky woman is." With that he went up closer to the young farmer. "You're not going to tell me it really is the Jewish girl?"

"Help!" Chane called out again, "Father Hilarion, quick!" Then she heard from behind her a strange, inarticulate sound, like a howl of fury from some beast, and when she turned round she saw Janko's axe poised above his antagonist's head.

At that moment the door was flung open and a young man in a cassock came rushing in. It was the priest's assistant who lodged in Janko's house. He had heard Chane's cry just as he was about to go into the presbytery

"God in heaven!" he exclaimed. "You, Janko?!" He tore the axe out of his hand and pushed the smith back. "Peace, you men, in God's name. What's going on here?"

No one answered. Janko was leaning against the wall, eyes closed, still deathly pale. But the smith seemed to have been struck dumb too. The sudden shock had sobered him up and his awe of the priest held his tongue in check. Although he was still young, Hilarion was highly respected in the village. He was a reasonable man who didn't expect his peasants to turn into angels overnight, but he did insist on correct behaviour in public.

"Well?" he asked in a severe voice, turning to Onufrij. "I suppose you've been teasing him again?"

"H-hmm." The smith cleared his throat in embarrassment. "But, Reverend Father, please, take a look at him.... The sheepskin jerkin, the cap, the axe—he's looking for a wife...and he comes here..."

Father Hilarion looked in bewilderment at his young landlord and then at the smith again. He clearly did not understand what the latter was driving at. When the penny did drop, his good-natured features flushed red with anger.

"Silence!" he thundered at the smith. "Have you no qualms about slandering a fellow Christian like that? To ask for the hand of a Jewish girl! Do you not know that is the greatest shame a Christian can burden himself with. He would be branded and condemned in this world and the next. I've long known you for a drunkard who loves to pick a quarrel, Onufrij, but I didn't think even you would go that far. Don't let me hear it again. You'll be in trouble if you spread this tale round the village. Do you hear?"

The smith bowed his head, full of remorse. "I won't repeat it," he assured the priest. "But it wasn't that bad—"

"A Jewish girl!" The priest interjected furiously. "There's no worse disgrace! Have you drowned what little Christian faith you have in schnapps? Love your neighbour as yourself! Damn and blast it, Onufrij, have you forgotten that?"

"No, of course not," the smith assured him. "But—what was I to think? Dressed like that, on a weekday—"

The priest cut him short. "What business is it of yours?" Then he turned to Janko, who was still leaning against the door, his eyes firmly shut, apparently in a daze, except that his hands were tugging convulsively at his belt. "Come on, Janko, tell us and put a stop to this malicious slander once and for all."

The young man twitched, opened his eyes wide and, a distraught expression on his face, stared at the priest, who was still holding the axe.

Father Hilarion assumed from the look he gave him that Janko wanted his axe back. Under the rod of their Polish overlords, under the aspergillum of the Jesuits, the Ruthenes, once such a warlike tribe, had become the mildest of the Slav peoples and only rarely took up that symbol of a free man. But once one had his axe in his hand, it was considered a great humiliation to let it be taken from him.

"There," the priest said, putting the handle into his hand. "Now tell us."

The Ruthene opened his mouth, but the only sound that came was a gurgle from his throat. He shook his head, turned round and staggered out of the door.

The priest watched him leave in bewilderment. "Strange," he said. "Something disagreeable must have happened to him. Perhaps he has to go to court to take an oath?"

He turned to Leib, who throughout this had looked almost as distraught as Janko, and addressed him in friendly tones. "You're a decent fellow, Leibko," he said, "can you tell us?" He often spoke of the little Jew in those terms, and really meant it. He had a high opinion of him and had no idea how deeply his reprimand to the smith had insulted him.

Leib gave a start. "Why he...?" he stammered. Must I lie? he thought to himself, horrified. Then, just in time, he felt the bony hand of his wife digging him in the ribs. "I...I..."

It was a good thing the priest was not looking at him. He was watching Janko out of the window. The young Ruthene was slowly heading towards his house, very slowly, head bowed, unsteady on his feet, almost stumbling, like a person who has just received a terrible blow to the head.

"So you don't know?" Father Hilarion asked. "Don't worry, I'll find out," he said, putting his hat back on. He turned to the smith. "And you can go home too. The father of a family wasting his money on drink! On a weekday! And I bet you've just borrowed it."

At this the smith drew himself up. "That's as maybe," he said in a mild but firm voice, "but it's no concern of anyone else's, not the Emperor's, nor the Pope's, never mind yours. What you said before was right, I'll stick to that, it's part of the Christian religion. But when I drink and how much I drink and where I get the money from for it has nothing to do with the Christian religion."

The priest looked as if he was preparing some riposte and stuck his hands on his hips. But he quickly let them drop again. As you like," he said, shrugging his shoulders. He realized he had gone too far. If he tried to stop his flock drinking, then they would stop obeying him in matters which even they agreed were the priest's business. "Just a friendly word."

After he had left, the smith settled himself in his seat again and ordered a third bottle. Leib slipped back into the kitchen to see his wife.

"Well, and what do you say to that?" he sighed. "I just hope Miriam didn't notice."

"No," she replied. "All she knows is that Janko had a tussle with the blacksmith. She doesn't believe he was drunk, but that doesn't matter. What do I have to say apart from that? That you're the biggest fool in Poland."

He did not ask why, he just mutely bowed his head in acknowledgment of his failings.

"You came very close," she snapped, "to ruining our daughter's whole life. Yes, I know, he wants to marry my daughter. If that happened, the priest would kick up a fuss that would be heard as far as away as Lemberg, not just in the sawmill in Halicz. God's been merciful to us—though you really don't deserve it—and seen that no harm's been done."

"You think so?" he asked timidly. "My heart is heavy. In his sheepskin jerkin and with his axe—that means he had marriage in mind! I never imagined he would be so serious about it."

"But that's just the point," she replied. "Now he knows what the priest and the other Christians think of it. If he's not completely mad, he'll be thoroughly ashamed of himself and won't show his face here again that soon."

Leib shook his head timidly. "But what if he is completely mad?" he asked, almost imploringly.

"Then they'll tie him up and take him to the madhouse," she said harshly. "Now leave me in peace."

5

The next day seemed to prove Chane was right. It was the first time for many years that Janko did not turn up on the dot of eleven. Leib was sitting behind the counter, heart pounding, starting at every step he heard outside.

Chane had found some work to keep Miriam occupied in the cellar, but after a while her red mane appeared in the taproom.

"What's going on?" she asked. "Yesterday he was supposed to be drunk and he's not come today?"

"Miriam!" Her mother's shrill voice rang out from the kitchen.

"Coming," Miriam replied, but she stayed there. "Father," she said, "you should go and see how he is. He might be ill."

"No," he mumbled. "But if you think…"

"Miriam!"

"Do go," she begged him and went out, leaving him with a new anxiety. She's so concerned about him, he thought. But then he took heart again. You old fool, he told himself. She's accustomed to him, why shouldn't she ask after him? He went back to listening for footsteps outside.

Finally the clock struck twelve and Janko still had not come. The village street came to life again as the people who had gone home for lunch returned to the fields. Janko was not among them. Leib went to stand in the doorway. He could not rid himself of his feeling of unease. He almost set off to see Janko, only his fear of what his wife would say held him back. It's not compassion, he told himself, but perhaps it would be a good idea to find out what he intends to do now. Of course the little Jew, who could not tell a lie to anyone else, was deceiving himself yet again. Despite his horror of the "animal" there was compassion in his feeling, genuine compassion. A peasant! Has been afflicted with this "love" as if Miriam were a Christian. Wants to marry her! A stupid peasant. But it must have been terrible for him yesterday, and today he may feel even more desperate. And had he not looked after this man for years? He had got into the habit of worrying about Janko. The next moment he was scolding himself for his weakness. No, it was nonsense. But still, it might be a good idea to...

One of the last to pass by on his way out to the fields was Janko's labourer, the redhead Saverko. When he saw the innkeeper he went over to him. "Hey, Yid," he said, "you know everything about the master, what's wrong with him? Is he going to be thrown off his farm? Since yesterday he's been sitting locked in his room, letting the farm look after itself. He's not eaten anything, he just sits there staring into space and muttering to himself. I think—" He tapped his forehead.

"And you're leaving him by himself?" Leib cried reproachfully.

"What can I do? Sit outside the locked door and keep guard on him in the cowshed? No one's going to steal him, for God's sake. I'm just telling you because you're his friend." With that he left.

For a second Leib stood there, undecided, then he hurried down the village street towards Janko's house, his little bow legs kicking up so much of the deep layer of dust that he seemed to be running in a cloud. He might try to do away with himself! Let Chane rant and rave, God wanted him to go to Janko...

Finally he reached the farm and hurried round the little house, in which Father Hilarion lived, to the cowshed, where Janko had partitioned off a tiny room for himself. The door was ajar. There was someone with him, thank God! He recognized the voice of the young priest.

"And I'm telling you," Father Hilarion was saying emphatically, "that she will not agree to be baptized. If you think that, you don't know that accursed race at all. They are born in blindness and remain so until they go down to hell. That is the curse our Lord has laid on them. And even if she did agree to be baptized, God preserve you from Jewish blood! They're all vindictive and grasping and dishonest. A stone is more likely to feel compassion than the heart of a Jew…"

He was speaking so loudly that Leib could hear every word, though Janko's mumbled response was inaudible to him. Then the priest's voice rang out again:

"No, the girl is not better than her fellow Jews. And even if she were, would the people in the village be willing to believe it? They would hate you and shun you even more than they do now, and with good reason. You'd have to give up your farm, to which you're so attached, and end up in misery with your Jewish wife and your Jewish children…"

Having listened this far, the little Jew slipped quietly away, afraid of being discovered. It was a relieved Leib that headed for the inn. He was not hurt by the vile things Father Hilarion had said about his race, his child. He was a Christian, how else should he speak of the Jews? The good thing was how vehemently he was warning Janko against continuing with his proposal; the man would not do anything silly now. Chane's fear, too, that Father Hilarion would kick up a fuss, was clearly unfounded. Since he was well disposed towards Janko, he would keep quiet for his sake.

Miriam was sitting on the bench outside the inn, mending one of her mother's dresses. When she saw her father approaching, she put her work down and went to meet him.

"Well?" she asked, a look of concern in her big brown eyes.

"He's all right," Leib replied. "He's just..."—got too much to do, was what he was going to say, but that would have been a lie—"having a discussion with the priest."

"At midday?" she asked in astonishment. "Is it because of his quarrel with Onufrij? But he'll come tomorrow, won't he?"

Again he felt the dark heat of apprehension rising up from the pit of his stomach. "Probably," he said falteringly, his eyes trying to pierce the expression on her fresh, coarse-featured face. "But if he doesn't, would that be a reason to be sad?"

She gave him a bewildered look. "What's happening?" she asked, grasping him by the hand. "Why doesn't he want to come any more. Of course I'd be sad. And you would too, wouldn't you? We both like him."

He gently withdrew his hand. "No, nothing's happened," he said, a little uncertainly, and went into the house. It's just that she's accustomed to him, he told himself again, looking, without any great success, for reassurance. Chane had set that afternoon for their trip to Halicz. He had resolved not to oppose her, though not to remind her, either. An old man like Reb David...it was a bitter pill. But now, with his last conversation with Miriam still fresh in his mind, he timidly murmured, "You said we should go and see Mendele..."

"Thank God you reminded me," she replied sarcastically, "otherwise I'd have forgotten such a trivial matter. Of course we're going.—Have you mended that tear, Miriam?"

Miriam brought the dress and helped her mother put it on. Leib stood wavering in the corner. "Get yourself ready," Chane snapped at him, but he stayed where he was until Miriam had left.

"Ought we to leave her by herself?" he asked tentatively.

"Of course. Is it the first time? As you can see, he's not coming back, probably doesn't dare. Anyway, he'll be out working in the fields now."

"He's not working," Leib replied. Then he drew himself up and said, with a firmness he had not managed for years, "We mustn't, Chane. You go by yourself."

She looked at him and immediately backed down, though in her own inimitable manner. She realized that this time he would not give way; perhaps he was even right. "It's the same old story with you," she scolded. "When you finally realize what you had in mind is a piece of nonsense, you bite my head off. Of course it's best if I go by myself, but how do you expect me to insist on it? You're always complaining I do the most important things without you…"

He breathed a sigh of relief. "I won't complain this time," he assured her in humble tones. "Anyway, you're the one who has to go, because you have to see the doctor. And since you'll be in Halicz," he went on, "you could have a word with Mosche too. It's only a week to the first of October. Try and get him to extend the loan, at least until we know whether Paterski's going to cancel the lease or not."

"That's what I had down as my first call," she replied. "But what can I say to him? Sweet talk won't get you anywhere with Mosche. And you—you brought this down—on us—all for the sake—of—of your friend—"

Once more she was overcome with a fit of coughing that

threatened to choke her. It was a long time before she could start out, and it was sheer willpower that kept her on her feet as she dragged herself along the dusty road. It took her a good hour to reach the little wood, and there she had to sit down and rest. I'll never make it to Halicz, she thought dejectedly, and how on earth am I going to get back?

Just as she was beginning to despair, help arrived in the shape of a long procession of carts, each loaded with one huge treetrunk. The Jewish carters walked alongside, cracking their whips. The foreman, Hirschele Krakauer, who worked for the Halicz sawmill, was sitting on the last cart. Chane knew him well and called out to him.

Hirschele stopped at once and made room for her beside him. He was a friendly man who liked a good chat. "Just the person," he said. "With no one to talk to your tongue could drop off for lack of use. So you're off to Halicz? Perhaps even to..." He screwed up his eyes and gave her a roguish wink.

"What do you mean?" she asked.

"Yes, it could be you they were talking about. Your Rosele's a fine girl—" he smacked his lips appreciatively "—and your husband's a *shenker*, too. Though how long he's going to keep the lease to the inn..."

"Stop beating about the bush, Reb Hirschele, and say what you have to say," she said sharply. "I wish you no worse worries than my Leib has about how long he will retain the lease. And my daughter's called Miriam. But what are you driving at?"

He gave her a searching look, but her expression remained blank. "Well, they must have been talking about some other girl," he said. "I'd have been pleased for you if it had been your Miriam, but I thought it was unlikely right from the start. A lovely girl is what the old man is after, but with your daughter he'd get the two of you into the bargain." Then he told her that Mendele Shadchen had been coming to see his boss, Reb David, quite often recently. One of the other workers had overheard their conversation the previous day and told Hirschele about it before he set off that morning. It concerned the daughter of a village innkeeper. "So when I saw you on the road, I immediately thought, she's off to see Mendele, so as not to let her good fortune slip out of her grasp."

"Brilliant deduction!" she mocked. "A mother who has a girl like mine can wait for the *shadchen* to come to her. Anyway, the story's a lot of nonsense, a man like you, Reb Hirschele, shouldn't be repeating such gossip. That Mendele's been to see your boss, yes, I can quite believe that, he's there like a shot the moment he gets a sniff of a piece of business. But Reb David will have thrown him out. A man of seventy who buried his third wife only six weeks ago…"

"That's what you think, is it?" Krakauer crowed. "My friend heard every word. 'That's suits me fine,' Reb David said, 'I know the girl. You sort the matter out,' he said, 'and I'll be quite happy to cough up a hundred crowns for the old folks too, if necessary.' And why shouldn't he do that? Do you think at seventy a man has time to wait? Should he get himself an old woman for his last pleasure on earth?"

Chane heart was pounding fit to burst. "If you say so," she said as impassively as possible. "But what's it to do with us?"

From then on it was Reb Hirschele who did all the talking. Although he went on and on about his master's wealth and the profitable business he was doing supplying the sleepers for the railway, for which the tree-trunks on the carts were destined, she hardly listened. God is merciful, she kept repeating to herself, now everything will be all right.

She got down and took her leave of Reb Hirschele as soon as they reached the first houses of Halicz. The cart would go past the "beauro" and he did not need to know where she was going, no more than Mendele needed to know in whose company she had come to the town. She had to go and see him first; it might make the visit to Moses Erdkugel superfluous.

When Chane entered the matchmaker's waiting room, she enjoyed a similar reception from Beile Pulverblitz as her husband had two days before. Only this time the fat woman did not get anywhere with her haughty approach.

"I should wait, should I," Chane asked, "until your husband has time for such a trivial matter? In that case he'll have to find the time to come and see me tomorrow." With that she strode past the astounded woman, head held high, and out of the door, only coming back in when Mendele opened the window and called out to her.

"Forgive us," he said, "but my wife knew that I've nothing to tell you yet. I'm so involved in important business at the moment—people are coming to me from a hundred miles away—that I—"

"That you," she interrupted, "went to see Reb David early yesterday morning to discuss it. Even before you knew we were agreeable!"

But Mendele Pulverblitz was not easily put off his stride. The thick lips pursed and emitted a low whistle.

"It seems you are not agreeable," he said in mocking tones. "You kept a watch to see if I'd been there just out of curiosity.

But Mendele Shadchen does not lie. I was there, but only on behalf of another prospective bride, who would bring me more than ten crowns. I think he's going to agree, but if that arrangement doesn't come off, I'll talk to him about your daughter."

"That won't be necessary," Chane replied, getting to her feet. "Reb David knows our daughter, and that's the one he wants, so we've no need of your services. We'll get someone else to talk to him who'll do it for nothing and we can keep all of the hundred crowns he's going to give us. A man who tells lies to try and extort more than has been agreed deserves to get nothing as punishment. God be with you."

This time something happened that few people had witnessed. Mendele Shadchen really did look abashed. But only for a moment. He was with Chane before even she had her hand on the doorknob.

"Is there any need for this?" he asked with a smile. "Now that I've arranged everything, you want to get someone else to complete the business. Is that fair? Sit down, Chane. You're an intelligent woman and I'm not stupid, we'll soon come to an agreement. Right then: Reb David agrees, the engagement contract can be drawn up as soon as you like, tomorrow even. But for the moment this all has to stay between ourselves. If you believe your Miriam can keep it to herself, then you can tell her the *tnoim* has been signed. If, however, you think she'll go boasting about it, then it's better she doesn't hear about it until later."

"Why?" Chane asked suspiciously.

"In the first place he wants to see his Nathan married beforehand. I've sorted out the engagement with the girl from Husiyatin. Your husband will have told you about it? The wedding's in four weeks' time, at the end of October. You can understand that he wants to keep his engagement secret until after that. A seventy-year-old father getting wed at the same time as his seventeen-year-old son? And both living under the same roof? It might look a little grotesque. And then, even when you're as old as he is and are therefore in a hurry, you don't get engaged six weeks after you've just buried your third wife. So: everything can be signed and sealed now, but the engagement will be announced just a few days before the wedding."

"And when will that be?" she asked.

"The middle of November. By then he'll have been in mourning for a full thirteen weeks. You can't ask more of a man who's seventy."

Chane thought for a moment. "Agreed," she said. "But now to our conditions. What provision is Reb David going to make for my daughter when—I mean if he should die before her."

Mendele made a show of being astonished, then indignant. "A bridegroom and you expect me to discuss his death with him?!" he exclaimed. But the next moment he had thought better of it. "I am sure he will live for many more years and the marriage will be blessed with children," he said. "However, you're right, we have to make provision for the opposite eventuality. Have you already worked out what you want to ask for?"

Again she stared into space, pondering her reply. "I'd prefer to leave that to our next meeting," she said after a while. "My husband has to have his say as well. But it won't be a small amount, I can tell you that now. She has nothing but a bit of youth and beauty, and that she's sacrificing to an old man. She won't inherit anything from us, she has to be provided for if she's left a widow on her own."

The matchmaker nodded. "If what you ask for is reasonable, he'll agree to it. But your own demands could be the rock on which the whole thing founders." He gave her a calculating look. "If I know you," he went on in a tone of honest indignation, "you'll be demanding at least three hundred crowns, when a hundred is probably the best you can expect. I'll have to wrestle with the old skinflint for every heller beyond that."

She stared at him in astonishment, but then she realized what he was getting at. "In your opinion" she said, "how much should we ask for, and what are your conditions?"

"Three hundred crowns," he said with an imperturbable smile. "Ten per cent for me, that is thirty crowns, meaning I'll get forty crowns in all from you. You're a tough bargainer, Chane! If it had been your husband…"

"Enough of that!" she said vehemently. She could criticize Leib, but she alone, no one else. "What do you know of my husband!?" She was so angry, he had difficulty calming her down, but before she left they agreed she would send word the next day, Thursday, and would get his reply by Sunday morning. If everything went according to plan, the engagement contract could be signed in his office on Sunday afternoon.

Head held high, she went out into the street. She could go home now. She'd ask the doctor another time, that could wait. And there was no need to go and see Moses Erdkugel at all, that would sort itself out once the engagement had been announced.

The feeling of euphoria filled her ailing body with new vigour and she made her way quickly through the little market town. But still it was good that she was overtaken by a carriage from Vinkovce as she was passing the last houses. In it was a small, skinny old man with a suspiciously glazed look in his eyes; the hand holding the reins was trembling too. It was Harasim

Kozarczuk, the mayor of Vinkovce. Chane called out to him and it was not his doing that the horse only stopped after it had gone on for a fair distance. It was as if the intelligent stallion was well aware that responsibility for their safe homecoming lay on it alone. When its master was in this kind of alcoholic stupor it didn't pay much attention to what he said or did.

"Did you see that?" the old man moaned when Chane, panting, reached him, "Not even my horse obeys me any more. Get up," he said, shifting to one side. "A drive with an old Jewish woman isn't exactly what you'd call a pleasure, but a poor decrepit old man has to put up with that, and worse. Gee-up!" The horse set off. "Yes, Chane, what a life I have! And why?" He began to sob. "Just because I'm the mayor."

Chane knew how to handle him when he was like this. "Yes, Harasim," she said, "you have a hard time of it. But what in particular have you had to put up with today?"

"Don't ask me," he whined. "It's too much.... Just recently I got a letter from the Emperor's official in Halicz—the man keeps on writing to me, just to annoy me, even though he knows I can't read—and Father Hilarion said to me, 'Mayor,' he said, 'it says here you have to go to Halicz on Wednesday, you and the mayors of the other villages the iron horse is going to pass through, because of the railway.' Like a fool, I was glad it was nothing worse, and the elders I consulted were glad too. We thought every village was going to get compensation, for having to put up with the stench and the black magic. 'Demand a thousand crowns for Vinkovce,' they said, 'or ten thousand. As much as the other villages.' Well then, at ten o'clock there we all were, in the magistrate's office, and he started to speak. 'The iron horse,' he said, 'is not black magic, but a machine. And there's no demon inside it,' he said, 'nor a damned soul either, but a boiler…' and all sorts of nonsense like that. And he wants us to tell everyone! Well you just keep on talking, brother, we thought, we won't actually do it, because every child in the village would laugh us to scorn, but presumably now you're going to hand over the crowns. That seemed to be right, because now he started telling us, 'The iron horse is a blessing for every country, everyone will profit from it and no one suffer harm, and therefore—' And what do you think he said? Oh, the bitter disappointment!" The drunk mayor started sobbing again.

"Well?" Chane asked.

It was a long time before Harasim could carry on. "'Therefore everyone should be in favour of it,' the magistrate said, 'and not make difficulties,' he said, 'and in particular no one whose fields the iron horse is going to run across should even think of asking more than the usual price for the patch of land. And if he does ask for more,' he said, 'then he'll make the Emperor very sad, because he likes the iron horse, but it won't do him any good, because there will be a Commission to value the land and he will only get his due and no more.' And they make an old man go specially to Halicz for that, Chane! 'Prepare your people,' he said. 'Soon we'll be coming to arrange everything.' Oh, oh…"

"Oh, that's hard," she said, just for something to say. In her mind she was far away, in the future. She saw her daughter as mistress of a wealthy household, an old man's wife, it was true, but free from care, content, envied by all.

At that same moment the little innkeeper was sitting at the taproom window staring out into the twilight and viewing his daughter's future in a very different light. Janko had not shown his face again, perhaps, cowed by the priest's vehement remonstration, he would not come back at all. Perhaps! But Leib felt that was more a hope than an expectation. That Janko, he thought to himself, he's as stubborn as a mule, once he's got an idea into his thick skull, he'll follow it through to the bitter end. Again he saw the gleam of the axe he'd seen in his dream. He had told himself the dream had simply been a presage of the clash between Janko and the smith, but he was not entirely convinced.

Then the man entered who had just been on the edge of his thoughts: Onufrij the smith, together with some of the elders of the village, who intended to wait there for the mayor's return. Leib had to light the oil-lamp hanging from the ceiling and bring schnapps for them. The room began to fill up more and more, so that Miriam had to help serve them. When she came in, the corners of Onufrij's lips twitched in a repressed smile, but he said nothing. Later on he called out, "Well then, Leibko, when're you going to find a husband for your daughter? A Jew isn't good enough for her, I suppose?" but only Leib understood what he was referring to. It made him start, but the smith took it no further. "Schnapps!" he roared, "today it's our Emperor who's paying," and the rest joined in with shouts and cheers. By the time it was dark and the mayor's carriage stopped outside the inn, Leib Weihnachtskuchen was the only sober and despondent man in the room.

That changed, of course, when old Harasim came staggering in, weeping bitter tears, followed by Chane. One look at her cheered Leib up immediately. She must have got Moses Erdkugel to agree to an extension, perhaps even had a promising report from Mendele; whatever it was, she brought good news. Her head was held higher, her look more assured than he had seen in his sick, embittered wife for a long, long time.

Of course, for the moment he could not ask her what it was. Even though Chane immediately set about helping him, he had his hands full serving the men. When they saw the mayor, all the villagers immediately cheered and ordered refills for their glasses. There was no reason for them to see the tears that were running down the mayor's cheeks as a bad omen. When a man from Vinkovce went to Halicz, he got drunk there, and when Harasim got drunk, he always cried. As he sobbed out his explanation, it took a long time before it sank in that he was bringing an acute disappointment for them all. Only a few were saddened at this, most grew angry. "The magistrate's a swindler!" some cried. "You can tell that from all his talk about boilers and machines. It's a barefaced lie!" Others declared, "Who's going to force me to sell my land if I don't want to? There's some dirty trick being hatched between the Poles and the officials behind it, they're always conniving with each other nowadays. We'll take it to the Emperor, he'll see we get justice." The most confident of all was the smith. "It doesn't bother me," he said. "Even if they can force me to sell the land beside my house for next to nothing, they can't force me to work for next to nothing—and what use is a smithy to them without a smith? Oh, the idiots!" And with a cry of triumph, he started singing a song, a round in which the rest all joined:

> Schnapps is worth its weight in gold,
> It's schnapps that makes us brave and bold.
> When the schnapps is drunk and gone's
> The moment when Old Nick will come.

It was close on midnight when the crowd began to thin out and Chane, who had sent Miriam off hours ago, went to bed herself. "I can't manage any more," she said. "I'll tell you about Halicz tomorrow. It's nothing but good news."

Leib nodded, elated. Her confirmation of his assumption gave him unaccustomed vigour, which even his customers noticed. "Look at Leib," one said, "he's skipping around like a little lamb. He doesn't believe the magistrate either, and he's a Jew."

"Huh!" said Onufrij contemptuously. "A stupid one, that's what he is. Any farmer's cleverer, and as for me—I tell you…"

And he told them for the tenth time how they had to send the *Kommissyja* about their business if they really did turn up in the village thinking they could get away with such an injustice. "We'll laugh at them till they pack their bags and leave."

It was getting on for two by the time Leib finally climbed into bed. But when the rays of the September sun lit up the room four hours later, he was already at his usual place with the *tefillin* wrapped round his forehead and arm. He found it comforting that it was Thursday, a day for which, as for Monday, different and longer prayers were prescribed than for the other four weekdays. Joyfully confident that all would now be well, he watched as the glowing ball of red emerged from the mists and rose in a glory of gold. "In Thee is my salvation. I trusted in Thee and Thou hast heard my prayer."

When, however, sitting in the taproom beside Chane after breakfast, he heard what her good news was, the joy disappeared from his soul and the light died in his little red-rimmed eyes. He hid his face in his hands, so she would not see his expression, and remained silent as she praised the Almighty for letting Reb David know Miriam already and Hirschele Krakauer come past with his cart at just the right moment. He had reconciled himself to this marriage, it had to be, and even the Lord God must have given it His blessing, otherwise He would not have allowed chance to intervene in such a miraculous fashion. But joy? No, he could not rejoice in it.

"Well, what do you say?" she asked, finally getting impatient. "You sit there as if the disaster had rendered you speechless."

"No, no," he said timidly, "it's not a disaster, but…it's not what I'd hoped for…" Watch out, he thought, now you'll feel the rough edge of her tongue.

But she remained silent, the only sound her heavy breathing. And when he looked at her, he saw two tears suddenly appear and roll down her haggard cheeks.

"Chane," he murmured and grasped her hand. He wanted to say something and found he couldn't, but there was a whole world of love and remorse in that one, tremulous word.

She understood. "Don't say anything," she said, her voice choked with tears. "It isn't our fault that we have no other way of providing for her."

"Not your fault," he murmured meekly, "but mine?"

"Don't go blaming yourself," she said, waving his scruples away. "We must remain calm, we're going to need all our strength. So, we're agreed we shall give her to Reb David?"

"Yes," he said in resolute tones, adding, rather more tentatively, "but of course we must ask Miriam first…"

She stared at him in amazement, as if she thought he must be going out of his mind. "Ask her first?" she repeated slowly, drawing out the words. "Whether she's willing?"

"I was only saying…"

"That is a crazy idea," she said tartly. "My father didn't ask me, nor yours you—nobody asks their children, unless it's a *daytsh* in Lemberg or Czernowitz who isn't a proper Jew any more. And that's why our marriages are happier than theirs. Is that true or is that not true?"

"It is true," he answered

"And what does the child know of life? She'll say no, partly because she'll want to stay with us longer and even more so because she'll be put off by the man's age. But does she know, the way we know, the kind of existence she's condemning herself to if she refuses?"

He bowed his head. He had spoken because he felt he had to, but his wife was right, and there were many other arguments against it as well. And yet! He felt as if there were two different persons inside him, one crying out, "She must decide herself," and repeating it while the other was warning, "It's against all tradition and reason." The first voice was louder, the second more insistent.

"Well?" she snapped.

"I just thought, because he's so old…"

"So you insist?" she asked, quivering with rage. "Just now I was trying to stop you feeling the life we have, the poverty and cares are all your fault. But if you insist on your crazy idea, then our daughter's misery will be your fault, and even the Lord God won't be able to relieve you of that guilt."

"Do not call on Him," he pleaded. "What He wants…I don't know what He wants in this case," he gasped in a torment of dread. "I just thought…I'm not insisting on it."

She was preparing another angry outburst, but she repressed it when she saw how deathly pale he was.

"In that case," she said, "Miriam will be told in four weeks time that she's to be married. Have you any objections to that?"

"No." He could no longer hear the two voices quarrelling so bitterly inside him, now just the one again, and it was saying, "At least let her remain the happy, innocent girl she's been so far for another four weeks."

"Now the conditions. How much should he settle on her? It's not easy to know what to ask for. He's rich, but he has lots of children. I think we can ask for a thousand crowns. No more, but no less."

"If you say so," he said meekly.

"Then her trousseau—we can't give her anything to take with her." Her voice quavered with a bitter undertone. "Only the basic essentials. If he's the decent man we think he is, he'll want to provide something better for his wife...say thirty crowns for a dress and some bodices."

His lips twitched, as if he too were swallowing a bitter pill. "It is necessary," he said softly.

"And finally, what do we ask for for ourselves?"

"For ourselves?!" he exclaimed, flushing bright red.

"Yes," she replied. "Why are you so surprised? When a rich old man marries the beautiful young daughter of poor people, it's customary for him to bestow something on his parents-in-law. Mendele thinks he can get three hundred crowns for us—if we give him ten per cent."

"Chane!" he cried in a hoarse voice, leaping to his feet. His face had reverted to its deathly paleness. "Chane! And you want to accept that?"

"Why not?" she asked. "It's so usual, he offered a hundred crowns himself straight away."

Leib Weihnachtskuchen wrung his hands. "Chane," he begged, "you don't mean that seriously—you can't mean it seriously.

Don't you realize what that money would be? The—" He could not bring himself to speak the words. "The—price for your own flesh and blood!" he cried.

"Nonsense!" she screeched.

But even louder, from the depths of despair, came his reply. "I will not sell my child. I will not...not..." His voice choked in a convulsive sob, he hid his face in his hands and slumped back onto the bench.

For a moment Chane said nothing. She was unaccustomed to such a loud, passionate outburst of distress from her normally meek husband. Also, in one corner of her heart a vague feeling stirred that it might not be nonsense after all. But it quickly passed. Why should they be better and wiser than the rest of the world? And what would happen to the two of them if she gave in?

She straightened up. "Don't shout like a madman," she said sharply, "and stop crying like a little child. Listen to me." And she explained that she was only following a generally accepted custom, naming other people who had done the same. "Do you want to give the money to Reb David?" she concluded. "And how are you going to pay Mosche then, how will you find a new livelihood for us?"

He had listened to her without moving. Now that he took his hands away from his face, she could see how pale he still was, even his lips were drained of blood. But there was no tremor in his voice when he said, "I will not do it, I will not allow it. Just now I thought it was He who was saying we should ask her. Perhaps I was mistaken, and if that was so, then He must forgive me. But what He is saying to me now I can hear as clearly as your voice, and He is saying, 'That must not happen, Leib, it was not for that that I blessed you with such a child, it would be sinful and shameful.' And that is why it will not happen."

He did not raise his voice, but the words came from his pale lips in a steady flow, like a solemn vow.

Once more Chane was at first struck dumb. Her anger at his obstinacy and horror at the consequences were like a noose tightening round her throat. When finally, with the strength of despair, she tried to free herself from it, she was overcome by the enemy lurking within her sick body

"And Mosche?" she cried. "And me? Because of you I've had a miserable life…but I insist on a proper deathbed…I don't want to die…in a ditch—" The last word was choked by a convulsion, her face twisted and blood-flecked foam stained her lips as she opened them wide to suck in air, as if she were in her death throes.

But what was perhaps even more terrible was that the same expression of mortal fear was on Leib's face. He swayed like a drunken man, the fingers of one hand clutching the table edge to stop him from falling. The other hand trembled as he raised it, as if to ward off evil.

"I cannot," he groaned, "I cannot."

Miriam had heard her mother coughing. Full of concern, she came rushing in and put her arms round her, so that she did not see her father's gesture. It was only when Chane, after she had got her breath back, gave him a baleful look, that she realized there had been yet another scene between the two. It had been like that for as long as she could remember: her mother scolded her father and her father tried to placate her or meekly accepted the scolding in silence. It was as much part of her life as Tuesday coming after Monday, not something she worried about. At most she felt a little sorry for her father, slightly more than she felt sorry for herself when she suffered the same fate, but only slightly. That morning, however, seeing him standing there with such a distraught expression on his face, for the first time in her life, she thought, he's so good, he always gives way to her, why is Mother so hard on him? Without thinking, she withdrew the arm she had put round Chane and her large, brown eyes turned to her father with a look full of love and pity.

He saw the look and, strange to say, the man who only understood Him, who looked on the world with the eyes of a child, immediately recognized what his daughter was thinking.

"No! No!" he exclaimed, as if to ward off the pity and excuse his wife. Then he heaved a deep sigh, shook his head and slipped out of the room.

6

He sat down on the little bench outside the house and stared into space. Whenever a villager passed, he bade him a deferential good morning; for Father Hilarion, who was going to the presbytery, he even stood up, though he was hardly aware of what he was doing. His whole being was turned inwards, listening and listening.... The was no doubt, it was His voice, and it said, "No!"

His head sank lower and lower onto his chest. He could not help himself, nor could he help his wife: His will had to be done.

He was still sitting like that when Miriam came out to find him. "Mother's writing a letter to Halicz," she said, "you're to come and read it before she seals it."

He stood up and crept into their little parlour. His wife did not look up. "Listen," she said grimly and read out the letter to him. In it she asked for a thousand crowns for Miriam and thirty crowns for her trousseau, adding that, assuming Reb David agreed to these main points, they would discuss the rest on the Sunday before the engagement contract was signed. "And now find someone to take it to Halicz," she said.

He stood there, irresolute. "I'll take it myself," he said finally. "But then on Sunday are we going to...?"

"That's enough," she said vehemently. "Not another word today, I'm completely drained."

Head bowed, he left her. The church clock was striking eleven as he went out of the house and Miriam came running after him.

"Father," she said, "do you think he'll come today?"

He started. "No," he gabbled, "I hope not..."

"But why ever not?" she asked. "Won't you tell me? Have you fallen out?"

"No.... Another time."

He tore himself away and left. She misses him, he thought with a quiver of concern. But that's not surprising, he reassured himself, she'd even miss a dog if it had come every day at the same time for that long.... And yet...if only she were married already, he couldn't help thinking. But would that ensure her happiness?

Once more his melancholy thoughts closed in on him. Suddenly he heard the loud crack of a whip behind him and jumped to the side. It was Hirschele Krakauer, by himself this time, and in a light carriage. "I bet you're heading for Halicz?" he asked with a sly smile as he stopped. "Come on then, hop in, it'll be an honour. But be quick about it. I had to go over to Jezupol at crack of dawn and this afternoon I've got to be with the men floating the timber down the Dniester again."

Eventually Leib managed to get a word in. "I won't come with you," he said, "but if you could take this letter for me...to Mendele Shadchen."

Hirschele laughed out loud. "You don't need to tell me who it's for. Consider it done. *Mazeltov!*" Still laughing, he drove off.

In consternation Leib watched him disappear. *Mazeltov!* The usual word for congratulations on an engagement! Only now did he remember what Chane had told him about Hirschele's suspicions the previous day. In an hour the whole of Halicz would know who Reb David was getting engaged to, and the old man wanted it kept secret! Leib wrung his hands. God of mercy, what had he done now? But it was too late, all he could see was the cloud of dust thrown up by the carriage. Soon even that had vanished.

Full of apprehension, he made his way back to the inn. What was he to say to Chane if she asked who was taking the message? She had had enough to get worked up about for one day already.

As he was about to go in, Father Hilarion came out of the presbytery and called over to him.

"Ah, Leibko, my good fellow," he said, "I need to talk to you. About Janko."

They went into the taproom, which was empty. When she heard the bell go as they entered, Miriam put her head round the door to the parlour but immediately disappeared again.

"It won't take long," the young priest said in a low voice. "You know what madness the devil's put into Janko's head? Well, what do you think about it?"

"Me?" said the little Jew. "I'm a Jew, my daughter's a Jew—what is there to say?"

Father Hilarion nodded. "That's what I thought. You'd rather she were dead than baptized, wouldn't you?"

Leib gave a start. "Dead?!" he mumbled in horror, stretching out a hand to ward off evil. "My...my only child..."

"I don't wish her any harm," the priest assured him. "I just meant that you would never allow her to be baptized. Yes? That's what I told Janko too, but you'll have to confirm it to him. As well as that, I persuaded him not to come here again, but only after I told him, 'The Jew demands that of you to repay him for everything he's done for you, so you have to agree.' But he says he wants to hear it from you, so go and see him this evening, when he gets home from the fields. He's working again today, thank God."

Leib promised. "Good," said Father Hilarion, getting to his feet. "But you'll stay firm, won't you? He might threaten you, but don't let that worry you. You have God and all the saints at your side."

The little Jew gave the priest a rather disconcerted look, but he did not notice.

"Because it is a good work, you see," he went on earnestly. "Pleasing in the sight of God. A Jewish girl should not become the wife of a Christian. That is not God's will, otherwise he would not have cursed you with such black souls.... You're a good man, Leibko, and I know your word is a solid as a rock, so I'm relying on you."

Leib went into the parlour to eat his meagre lunch with his wife and daughter. "The letter's gone," he said. Fortunately Chane did not ask who was taking it. She looked even more drained of colour and hollow-cheeked than ever. He noticed it and it grieved him sorely. The worry gnawed at him, but he could not regret his opposition to her proposal—His will must be done.

After Miriam had gone out he told her of the priest's request, hesitantly, since he was afraid it would get her worked up again. But she just nodded calmly and said, "Only we'll have to think up something to explain to Miriam why he's not coming any more. Otherwise the child will keep turning it over in her mind when she shouldn't be thinking of him at all. I'll work out something nasty he's supposed to have done to tell her this evening and say that's why we've banned him from the inn."

Leib felt uneasy. Thou shalt not bear false witness against thy neighbour, he thought. Out loud, however, he said, "What could that be? She's not stupid and she thinks well of him. Also that kind of thing is—forgive me—a sin."

Chane was about to fly into a rage, but at that moment a man came in who had not been seen in the inn for a long time: old Martin, Paterski's chief farmhand. "You're to come and see the master at once," he commanded.

Leib went pale. What new torment did his landlord, who was already angry with him, have in store? Chane, too, was filled with consternation, but she immediately recovered her composure, invited Martin to sit down and brought him a glass of their best brandy. Then she tried to worm some information out of him.

"No idea," he said, but smacked his lips contentedly as he emptied his glass and pushed it out in front of him. She took the hint and filled it. "Some kind of business, I think," he added. She filled his glass again, and he went on, "The master was in Halicz from yesterday morning until midday today, drinking with the officials. That always costs a lot, he only does it when he wants something out of them. Though what kind of business it was this time, I don't know. But he definitely got what he wanted, he was very pleased with himself when he got home. And straight away he ordered me to come here. The mistress was astonished, but he told her, 'I can't do it without that stupid little swine.' Yes," he concluded with a satisfied burp, "that's what he said. You should be glad."

And indeed, Paterski's reception of the little innkeeper, when he appeared before him, bowing and scraping, was very friendly. "Come over here, dogshit," he said. "I think you've been stupid rather than bad, so I've decided to give you another chance. It was ungrateful, grasping and mean—that is, Jewish—of you when you persuaded Janko to borrow money from the priest of Solince. But you were also stupid. What is more use to you, my goodwill, or the ten crowns reward for setting up the deal?"

"I only got two crowns out of it," Leib insisted. "And Janko gave me them of his own free will. I asked for nothing from the priest and he gave me nothing."

"Lies!" thundered the Pole. "And even if it is the truth, what then? You got nothing out of it, and Janko and I even less. Perhaps you'll start drivelling on about lower interest. Very well then, twenty per cent, but was that good advice? He might be able to squeeze that much out in a good year, but one bad harvest and your dear Janko is ruined. Anyway, he'll be in the priest's debt for ever. The sensible thing would have been to say to him, 'Sell a third of your land, then the rest will be almost free of debt.' But you were too stupid to think of that."

"I did," Leib assured him, "but he wouldn't listen. And anyway, who would have given him a halfway decent price—"

He broke off, aghast. He could hardly tell this nobleman to his face that, being the only person buying land in Vinkovce, he was forcing down prices in an outrageous manner. He had eliminated the competition: Moses Erdkugel by denouncing him to the authorities for usury and the Armenian by an agreement whereby the latter would buy nothing in Vinkovce and he, Paterski, nothing in Halicz.

"Who?" the Pole thundered. "Me, that's who! You know I'm ready to ruin myself when I get it into my head to round off my property. And since the subject's cropped up, I'm still prepared to do that. If Janko's willing to sell me the orchard beside his house, he can have the price, cash in hand, tomorrow. It borders on the orchard I've bought from Vassily Bukovich, that's why I'd like it.

He'll get a fair price. That damned priest—a priest and a usurer, it's a disgrace!—will have had everything valued. You'll have seen the valuation, was it too low?"

"No," said Leib, "it was fair."

"Well then, I'll pay that price, and a few crowns more if you like. You know me, Leib, when I'm set on something, I'm like a child. Actually, the reason I sent for you was another matter: I want to buy Onufrij's bill of exchange from the Armenian. But there's plenty of time for that, let's get the other piece of business over with first. Ten crowns for you if you can arrange it. And of course, you'll keep the inn too. But it has to be done quickly. If it drags on, the impulse will have passed and with it my willingness to throw my money away. Agreed?"

Leib was flabbergasted. Such a price and such a commission for arranging the deal! What had got into Paterski? But it was impossible.

"Your honour," he said hesitantly, "Janko won't do it. He's determined to keep the farm undivided. And the orchard he lavishes such care on would be the last bit he'd sell. Even a field's a better bet."

"You cur!" the Pole cried. "I offer you a lifeline and you refuse to help me?! Janko does what you tell him to—do you have the insolence to deny that? Woe betide you if you don't arrange it for me…. Actually, I would like to buy some farmland from him as well," he added in calmer tones, "but I must have that orchard, I've set my heart on that. Now off you go, and be sensible. You know I'm not a man to be trifled with."

A bewildered Leib told his wife about the strange commission. "There must be something behind it," he said.

For a long time she said nothing. What was behind it was immediately obvious to her: Paterski had found out in Halicz which land the railway was going to be built on, and it included Janko's orchard. But she couldn't tell her husband that or he would advise Janko against it. On the contrary, she had to make sure he did everything to get the farmer to agree.

"You fool," she said. "What's the point in racking your brains about what Paterski has in mind?! He probably wants to set up a large fruit plantation, that's why he's willing to pay that much. If you arrange it, you can save us from destitution, and it's a good deal for Janko as well."

"But he won't agree," Leib said.

"He must!" she cried. "Do the sensible thing for once in your life," she went on in pleading tones. "Think of yourself for once, and of me. Reb David wants to give us money—you say no. Paterski's willing to keep you in the inn and you're wondering whether it wouldn't be better for that ugly brute who's after your daughter if he kept the orchard. You always follow God's commandment, you say. Is it God's will that I should live and die in penury?"

He bowed his head. "I'll try," he promised. "I'll do what I can."

With that intention he set off, as twilight was falling, for Janko's house. The young Ruthene was sitting on the little bench outside his room eating his supper, a piece of polenta, and drinking from a jug of water. When he saw the Jew approaching, a quiver went through his sinewy frame and a flush appeared on his emaciated, careworn features.

"The priest's already told me," he growled, "but you're wasting your breath."

"Won't you listen to me first?" Leib begged.

Janko shook his head grimly. "What's the point?" he asked in dispirited tones. "I know how you feel and I know what you're going to say. But you don't know how I feel…. I miss her," the words came tumbling out, "I must see her or I'll go out of my mind!"

"But don't you see…it's impossible. You must forget the whole idea."

"Why?" the young Ruthene demanded. "I'm a man and she's a girl, I love her madly and she's always been kind to me. Impossible? Because she's Jewish? Is she a cow and I'm a horse? We're both human beings! And what is there that's Jewish about her? Not her face, nor her language, nor her habits—she's a villager like me. I tell you, Leibko, she's better suited to me than to one of your silly, pasty-faced young puppies with sidelocks. Why shouldn't she be baptized, why shouldn't I marry her? The priest is against it and you're against it, but what's that to us if it suits the pair of us? The priest says the villagers will look down on me even more than they do now. I don't give a damn! Or because you won't stand for it? You will stand for it when I tell you she's going to be my wife and no one else's. If you get her engaged to someone else, I'll kill her then kill myself."

"Janko!" Leib exclaimed. He had tried in vain to interrupt him. The words the man had been brooding over for days came pouring out, in a rush, like pent-up waters when the dam bursts. "Janko! Is that your gratitude?"

"I'll only do it if I have to," Janko cried. "If I have my way, she'll live and be happy. I'll take her as she is, as my lawful wedded wife. I'll look after her as long as I live and may this hand wither if I ever hit her. Isn't that gratitude enough for you? Is it my fault you're not willing? A Jewish girl as wife is good enough for me, but a Christian man as son-in-law's not good enough for you. What can I do about that?"

"Not good enough, no, it's not that," Leib hurriedly protested, "it's just that it's impossible. I hoped you would see that. And you promised Father Hilarion you wouldn't come to the inn any more if I asked you."

"Yes," he replied, "but you shouldn't insist on it. Where will it get you? Do you think I'll forget her? It'll only get worse. I…I haven't got the words to describe it, but the last days, nights—" He clenched his teeth then forced the words out. "It can't be worse in hell. You're fools to insist on it, I'll only stick to it as long as I can, and that won't be very long…" He put his hand to his brow. "Not long before…" he said, distraught, "before I come and take her in my arms and say, 'You're mine, mine.' Madness, you say? Then I am mad—don't let it get that far. I just want to be able to see her, to talk to her, then I'll be sensible. As God is my witness, I won't say anything to her. Not a word, not a look—don't you believe me?"

"Yes," Leib said hesitantly, "I believe you really do mean that promise, but you'd find it impossible to keep it. Don't you see, it would only be adding fuel to the fire. You must forget her."

"Never!" was the young Ruthene's passionate response. "Never will another woman become my wife, nor another man her husband. If you refuse to let us live together, then we'll die together."

He pulled himself up to his full height, his yellowish complexion was suffused with blood, his timid eyes flashed. Almost mechanically his right hand went up, thumb, index and middle finger raised, indicating an oath. "Hear me," he declared.

"Many years ago, when I was little more than a child, I made a vow before the Lord God: this farm shall remain mine, not one speck of soil shall ever belong to another. And I have kept that vow, even though I had to work harder than the ox that pulls my plough and had a worse life than my dog. And today I swear: Miriam shall be mine. Alive or dead, that is your choice. And now go."

Leib was going to speak, but Janko repeated vehemently, "Go!" and so he made his gloomy way home.

Chane scolded him when he told her what had happened, but suddenly the stream of harsh words stopped and she stared thoughtfully into space.

"That can't be the end of it," she said slowly, "otherwise—" she cleared her throat "—otherwise there really will be a disaster. What these people call 'love'—ugh, disgusting!—but when one of them has caught this 'love' then it's often very dangerous if he's suddenly prevented from seeing the girl.... Perhaps it would be better if we allowed him to come here again. You believe he's an honest man, in which case he'll presumably keep his word."

Leib stared at her in astonishment.

"As far as he's able," he objected timidly. "In this 'love' they all behave like madmen.... And then there's Miriam—God forbid I should think her capable of anything wrong, but she keeps asking after him. For that reason alone it would be better if she got out of the habit of expecting him. Yes, she needs to forget him."

"Nonsense!" came the shrill interjection from Chane.

God grant it is nonsense, thought Leib. Out loud he said, "All right then. Perhaps it doesn't matter as far as she's concerned. But if he's here all the time, he might pick up a hint of the secret engagement. And when it's announced in five or six weeks time, he'll hear about it straight away. How are you going to protect her from him then?"

She dismissed his concern. "We'll deal with that when the time comes," she said, adding firmly, "So that means he can come back from tomorrow."

But Leib shook his head. "I beg you," he pleaded, "don't. Remember my dream. I wouldn't be able to relax for a moment…and even if there is no danger…" He broke off, a blush spreading over his wrinkled face.

"Well?" she bellowed at him.

But he had to take a deep breath before, cheeks burning and eyes fixed on the floor, he managed to stammer bashfully, "Now, Chane…now that we know what he wants and the way he thinks of her…I couldn't bear to watch him eyeing my daughter, touching her with his looks…"

"Fool!" she exclaimed. "Looks! Since when have looks been able to besmirch anyone? Right then, tomorrow morning you'll talk to Janko. Or…perhaps it's better if I do it myself."

"You?!" he exclaimed in a low voice, flabbergasted. "You?!" he repeated, drawing out the word, hoarse, all the colour draining from his cheeks, his stare becoming more and more fixed. A terrible thought, alarming even, seemed to have taken hold of him.

"You?!" he cried for the third time, almost shouting out the word as he grasped her hand.

"What's all this again?" It was meant to sound angry, but came out as disheartened. "Why shouldn't I?"

He stood up, pale as a sheet. "That will not happen," he said slowly, in a loud voice. "I forbid you, I, your husband, a poor man, but one who loves his child and fears Him. You were going to tell Janko that he can come here and caress my daughter with his lascivious looks, if he will sell his orchard to Baron Paterski."

She tried to speak.

"Do not deny it!" he thundered. Never before in all the long years they had been together had he spoken to her in that tone. "That was what you were going to do. You were hoping to use his madness to get him to agree to the deal. A clever scheme, but I am still alive and I say, no, no, no!"

Hot tears were pouring down Chane's cheeks. "Now you're accusing me of behaving like a bawd!" she cried, beside herself. "It's your foolishness, your weakness that has got us into this wretched state. It's your fault our child has to be sacrificed to an old man, it's your fault we're lost if the old man doesn't take pity on us. And when I try to do something to relieve our misery, our shame a little, so that we can at least continue to earn our own keep, you pour abuse on me!"

Leib's eyes were filled with tears too. "Chane," he said, trying to take her hand, "we are two poor people who have been brought low; let us live in peace together, instead of pushing each other down farther. Accuse me, if you want, if it eases the burden for you, justly or unjustly, I will not defend myself. Just one thing though: you must never again cause me the pain of having to speak to you as I did just now. I know you did not mean any harm and would rather die ten times over than than do anything you think would bring dishonour on your child. Looks, you say, what are looks? But I say to you, no decent Jewish woman should expose her daughter to looks like that to gain some advantage."

"So I'm not a decent woman?"

"Oh, but you are," he cried. "When the time comes for my

soul to stand before the Judgment Seat, I will say to Him, 'You laid many a heavy burden on Your servant on earth, but Your mercy was infinitely greater, for You gave him three blessings: the ability to perceive Your will, and this wife and this child.' You are different from me, Chane, but I know you are a good woman. Behaving like a bawd?!" He raised his hands in horror at the idea. "God forbid, Chane, not you, but poverty and worry, they are the bawds, and He alone knows why He has let them become so great here on earth. It is they who lead people astray, they who turn people to evil, but we must remain on the path of righteousness. You meant no harm—but we are Jews, we must have greater regard to ourselves and to the purity of our children than the others, for we are His people. As well as that, it would be deceiving Janko, and one should not deceive anyone, least of all a man who is blinded by 'love'."

"Oh, don't go on," she said, half angry, half ashamed. "We're still talking at cross-purposes. That's another way out you've cut off."

"With His help we'll find a better one," he said in reverent tones and went outside.

For a long time he walked up and down in the dark night, prey to conflicting feelings. On the one hand he felt sadness at having had to speak so harshly to his sick, careworn wife; on the other satisfaction at having remained firm. But that feeling contained no trace of pride, he bowed his head humbly before God. How was it possible, he wondered, that I found such words. It was He who put them in my mouth, blessed be His name.

While he was standing there in the dark, the pain in his heart gradually easing, he suddenly heard a noise in the quiet of the night. It was like a faint, distant shuffling. He pricked up his ears. The sound grew louder and clearer; someone was creeping along the road towards the inn, with hesitant steps, stopping all the time. Leib could not recognize the person from the silhouette, but when the figure stopped once more, only twenty yards away from him, and sighed deeply, he began to suspect who it was. Holding his breath, Leib tiptoed to the door of his house. He was about to go in and close the door behind him, but a strange feeling, a mixture of pity and dread, kept him fixed on the threshold.

The young Ruthene came nearer and nearer until he was standing close to the house. "She's already asleep," Leib heard him say, "Everyone's gone to sleep. I'm the only one who can't."

A shiver ran down Leib's spine. Again he started to close the door and again the feeling stopped him. Then he decided to go up to the young man and speak to him, but for a long time he found it impossible. Finally he murmured his name.

Janko started. "Who...who's there?" he said, his voice unsteady. "Is that you, Leibko?"

The little Jew stepped out. "Yes, it's me. You should go home, Janko," he said gently. "You've a day's hard work in front of you tomorrow, you'll have to go out early."

"What's the point?" said Janko dully. "I don't want...I must..." Then he suddenly started crying and felt for Leib's hand. "Leibko," he sobbed, "dear Leibko, you were always like a father to me, have pity on me. Let me come tomorrow, I want to see her just for a minute."

"I can't," Leib said, "and it wouldn't help you either. Come, Janko, I'll walk home with you. We must have a proper talk."

Gently, holding his hand, he led him away. There was no talk, however. They walked along together in silence until they came to Janko's farm.

"So you won't let me?" Janko asked, his voice still unsteady. "Then may God have mercy on us all."

"He will," Leib replied in firm, heartfelt tones. "Goodnight, Janko." And he hurried off home.

The next morning, the Friday, while Chane and Miriam were in the kitchen preparing for *shabbes* and Leib was alone in the taproom, no fewer than four important messages came for him.

The first, and the only bad one, he had straight from the horse's mouth. The day had hardly dawned when Baron Paterski himself turned up at the inn.

"Well," he asked expectantly, "do I get the orchard?"

Leib folded himself into a humble posture. "Your honour," he said in a tremulous voice, bowing all the time, "I can't do anything. I haven't even managed to discuss it with him…"

"Cur!" Paterski screamed in fury, raising his riding crop. "You have the audacity to tell me that?"

Leib drew back. "Not for want of trying," he insisted. "But even before I could get round to mentioning the deal, he reminded me of his oath not to sell one single square foot of his land. As I said, it was while we were talking about something completely different."

"What was this other thing you were talking about?" Paterski asked, taking a step towards him, his whip still raised.

Again Leib drew back. "That I can't tell you, but, as God is my witness, it has nothing to do with the orchard."

"You're lying, you swine," the Pole cried, and this time the whip came whistling down, Leib only managed to avoid it by hopping into the doorway to the neighbouring room.

Paterski was breathing heavily. "It seems to me," he said in a voice thick with menace, "you're playing a double game. Has someone else given you the same commission?"

"No!" Leib assured him, adding in a tone of surprise, "Someone else? Why should people suddenly be keen to buy Janko's orchard?"

The Pole bit his lip. "I wouldn't know," he said eventually. "I just thought…because it's well known a Jew may be up to any crafty trick. So you refuse to do anything about it?"

"I can't, your honour. He won't sell."

"Then you must make him," Paterski snarled angrily. "You must! D'you hear? Just you listen to me, Jew. If by this evening you come and tell me I've got the orchard, no matter what the price, and that the business can be transacted in Halicz on Monday, then you can stay in the inn and I'll give you twenty crowns commission, or even thirty if you like. If you don't, then the lease will be cancelled at New Year and you'll be thrown out next summer, even if the Lord God himself should beg mercy for you. Good morning."

And he left.

Leib watched him go, bewildered and in sombre mood. Thirty crowns! By Monday! What ever was going on? But there was no point in racking his brains over that. One thing was certain, he wouldn't be staying in Vinkovce for much longer.

While he was still wondering whether to tell Chane about the conversation or keep quiet, another visitor entered. His behaviour towards Leib was no less haughty than the Polish nobleman's, even though he was so different from the latter it would be impossible to imagine a more complete contrast. It was a *shnorrer*, one of those Jewish travelling folk who are forever criss-crossing eastern Europe and often enough make their way to Germany and even America, from where they return to Galicia and Russia, a real plague on their fellow Jews. Many are dissolute riffraff, some simply beggars, others not without education and talents—you often come across able Talmudists, musicians and preachers among them—but all alike are hungry, thirsty and brazen.

"*Sholem aleichem*," he said as he entered. "Are you Leib, the *shenker*?" His accent betrayed his Russian origin.

Leib returned his greeting with a sigh. "*Aleichem sholem*. Yes, the innkeeper, that's me."

His visitor did not look very prepossessing. His filthy kaftan hung in tatters on his scrawny, wiry frame, his hat consisted of nothing but holes and all his worldly goods were stowed in a handkerchief tied to a stick. What dismayed Leib most was the red nose in the middle of the creased face with its unkempt beard. It is the custom, hallowed by tradition, that no devout Jew can let such a guest depart without offering him sustenance of some kind. And if he arrives on a Friday morning one must keep him, if he so desires, in the house over the day of rest until Sunday morning. It is seldom a pleasure, especially when the guest has such a nose and the host is an innkeeper.

"Sit down," said Leib. "Would you like something to eat?"

The *shnorrer* gave him a haughty look. "Why are you pulling a face like that?" he asked. "Do you think I want to spend *shabbes* with you? I am, thank God, used to better. And Reb Schlome in Jezupol—the richest man in the town—has invited me for this evening. With an invitation like that you don't stay with Leib

Shenker. I can do without your mouldy bread, too. Just give me a glass of schnapps, but your best, d'you hear. I am Reb Morche Kremmenitzer and I have a right to expect it."

Leib had never heard the name, but he did as he was commanded.

The *shnorrer* emptied the glass in one gulp and smacked his lips. "That's the real stuff," he said. "That's schnapps and not water. No wonder you're still such a poor beggar, Reb Leib... . Another glass."

Leib gave him another glass and even tried to look pleased. His guest had promised to leave soon and that deserved a reward.

This was followed by a third and fourth glass. At the same time the stranger ordered a snack: two hard-boiled eggs and some bread and butter. Obediently Leib went into the kitchen and brought what had been requested.

After the *shnorrer* had emptied his fifth glass, he stood up. His nose was a little redder, but he was steady on his feet.

"You're a good man, you do your duty," he said condescendingly, "and that deserves a reward. I have here a letter for you from Reb Mosche. The niggardly wretch gave me two kreutzers and said, 'That's for delivering this letter. It contains good news, so Reb Leib will look after you well.' But I said to myself, this Reb Leib will look after me well because I'm a guest. If he's stingy I won't give him the letter. There's something good in it—should I repay evil with good? You've earned it, here it is."

The Russian handed over the letter and left. With his heart in his mouth, Leib broke the seal and read it. He could hardly believe his eyes but yes, in the Hebrew script, with all its little flourishes, it actually said:

Dear Friend,

I hope you did not take what I said to you on Monday seriously. As you realized, I was in a bad mood, but it would never occur to me to do something that would inconvenience an old friend. I beg you to forgive me the distress I may have caused you. It will be a pleasure for me to extend your loan for as long as you want.

Mosche

Delighted and astonished, Leib stared at the letter. Then he ran into the kitchen. "Read that," he cried, handing the letter to his wife. Her careworn features briefly lit up with a shimmer of joy. But then she asked, "What's going on? Mosche's suddenly your friend and didn't mean what he said on Monday?"

"That's what it says there," he said happily, "so it must be true."

She shook her head. "He'll have heard about the arrangement with Reb David," she replied, sounding worried. "That's not good. Reb David wants it to remain a secret, he might even end up denying the whole business. But who could have spread the word?"

Leib went pale and trembled. She gave him a puzzled look. "Who did you get to take the letter to Mendele yesterday?" she asked.

He was so overcome with fear and remorse, he had to lean against the wall and instinctively shut his eyes. Pale-lipped, he confessed, "Hirschele."

"*Shlemiel!*" she exclaimed with a shrill cry. "Your bungling's ruined us all!" And a storm of reproaches rained down on him.

Head bowed, he let it wash over him without venturing a word in his defence. Not that any occurred to him; Chane was right, he was a *shlemiel*, his incompetence was the cause of their misfortune. Wearily he shuffled out, once she had exhausted herself with scolding, and sat down on the bench outside. This time he could not find comfort anywhere; in their dire situation even the thought of Him failed. Was it He who had commanded him to get the letter delivered by Hirschele Krakauer of all people?

He was still sitting there, staring gloomily into space, when he heard his name called. Standing before him was a strange little man in a threadbare kaftan. His diminutive stature and delicate limbs suggested a boy, but his ugly face had thousands of wrinkles and there were white threads in his ginger beard. It was Meyerl Spazierstock, Mendele's assistant and messenger. He was also his scout and spent most of his time going round, searching out the names and circumstances of those in need of a spouse anywhere within a sixty-mile radius.

Everything was swimming before Leib's eyes and the little man's grinning face appeared to him as if through a mist. Now Mendele's going to cancel the deal, he thought, shuddering at the consequences.

But Meyerl was clearly making an effort to put on as friendly an expression as possible. "How are you?" he asked. "And how is our lovely fat bride getting on?"

"Fine, thank you," Leib stammered. "What have you got for us?"

"Good news, of course." Little Meyerl threw out his chest. "When we take something on, everything goes smoothly. But what got into you to tell other people? Reb David was very angry. But we said to him, 'Who's bothered about gossip? And if anyone should ask you, you can always say it's news to you. Reb Leib and his wife will say the same, we'll make sure of that.' After that he calmed down. That's Mendele's message."

Leib gave a sigh of relief. "So that's why you've come?" he asked. But even he was not so naive as to believe that. "That's the only reason?"

"Of course," Meyerl replied. "And then—of course—because of the conditions. So...but I think your wife should be present as well, shouldn't she?"

Beaming with delight, Leib fetched her from the kitchen. Chane, despite her inner rejoicing, could not resist whispering to him, "You're still a *shlemiel*. And I decide on the conditions."

He did not argue and listened in silence while Chane managed to secure the thousand crowns widow's portion for Miriam and fifty, instead of the original thirty, crowns for her trousseau, since she correctly interpreted Meyerl's appearance as proof that the old bridegroom was keen to have the matter settled as quickly as possible. Leib only began to feel uneasy when Meyerl went on to say, "And what are your demands for yourselves? You say you want to discuss that on Sunday. Why wait until then? Is that convenient for Reb David and for you? I've a proposal: you get four hundred crowns and give Mendele fifty and me ten. But you must agree now, and thank me for my pains."

But they did not. His face flushed deep red, Leib squinted across at his wife. She, too, was silent as she worked out what the situation was. So that was why Meyerl had come, they'd already got the old man to agree to the four hundred crowns. "Four hundred," she said, "but only forty for the two of you."

"No!" Meyerl exclaimed. "I'd rather the deal fell through. Denying a poor man his hard-earned reward—"

"Silence," Leib broke in. "We will tell Reb David ourselves on Sunday whether we are going to ask for anything." And when Chane was about to start up again, he repeated in almost imperious tones, "Silence."

But this time she refused to be browbeaten. "We will go to the rabbi and let him decide," she said. "Do you know what he wants?" she asked, turning to Meyerl, as if looking to him for support.

But that did not trouble Leib; in this matter he obeyed His voice. "I want nothing," he said. "You can tell everyone." And he strode out of the room.

Meyerl watched him leave, flabbergasted. "Has he gone mad?" he asked. Chane shrugged her shoulders. "We'll work something out," she said, but she did not sound very sure. Then they arranged that the engagement contract should be signed at Mendele's house on the Sunday morning, since they would have to be back by Sunday afternoon, that being a busy time at the inn.

Once Meyerl had left and Leib came back into the room, she began to bombard him once again. Was he really counting on Mosche's generosity?

"No," he said, "on Him. And it's no use going on about your rabbi. I am so clear about what He wants that ten rabbis couldn't make it any clearer. My soul too has gone up into Mount Sinai and heard His voice."

She remained silent. Arguments of faith would get her nowhere here. The power of the rabbi is immense as far as the thousands and thousands of commandments and prohibitions in matters of ritual are concerned. In questions of conscience he has less power than any other priest. The soul of every Jew has "gone up into Sinai"; every individual feels close to his God and has no need of a mediator between him and his Lord.

7

The fourth arrival came at about midday, though this one was not unexpected. Ever since Leib and Chane had kept the inn in Vinkovce, long tall Kasia from Halicz had been coming at Friday lunchtime and staying until Sunday morning. She was their *shabbes goy*, the Christian servant who did everything their religion forbade to do on the sabbath, that is, put out the lights, serve the customers, receive or hand out money. For many a needy Christian woman in the east such poorly paid employment is often the only bright spot in a life of misery. However much they starve and freeze during the week, on the Jewish sabbath they eat their fill and are nice and warm, for on that day every Jewish parlour is heated and the table in it laid with a festive meal, even if the people have to stint themselves during the week or beg for coppers on the Friday to scrape enough together for it. That is why all the efforts of certain priests and officials to make the *shabbes goy* a thing of the past have been fruitless. The Jews need her and she needs them. There is fierce competition for every such post, even with the poorest Jews, especially since the work is light and the *goy* is well treated. Disputes are extremely rare and the relationship between mistress and servant is often a warm and friendly one, despite the immense contrast in outlook, despite the fact that each is convinced the other is a lesser mortal for the simple reason that she does not have the right faith. Despite all this, the *shabbes goy* is, and feels herself to be, part of the family and gradually learns the customs, even the language of her employers.

Kasia was a match for all her fellow *shabbes goys* in Podolia as far as loyalty and what some people called "going Jewish" were concerned. Countless Fridays had passed since that first one when Chane, still in the flower of womanhood, had chosen the young washerwoman from a whole host of applicants to serve the Weihnachtskuchen household. She chose her because she felt so sorry for the scrawny beanpole with the ugly, square face. All the women needed the position, but she most of all. A washerwoman—that is an occupation which is entirely dependent on the standards of cleanliness that obtain in the country, which is why in Podolia it is a passport to a life of unwanted leisure and hunger. Chane knew what she was doing when she chose the Halicz washerwoman and she never had cause to regret it. Kasia was quick to learn, and during the day when she was alone in charge of the taproom she attracted customers who would otherwise not have come to the inn. The attraction was not her body, but her mind: the Vinkovce gossips were delighted to hear from her what had been happening during the week in Halicz, and this all the more because her sabbath employment had the opposite effect from her work during the week. In her hands, the events in Halicz did not become any cleaner, they even became more colourful, as you might say.

There was a sundial on the church in Vinkovce, but the villagers did not need to see the shadow approaching XII to know that it was getting on for midday. An even more certain sign was Kasia, leaning forward and swinging her long arms as she hurried toward the inn. Today she was in an even greater hurry than usual, she was positively running, making her threadbare yellow shawl flutter like a flag round her bony shoulders. "What good fortune," she kept muttering to herself. "No *naden*. On the contrary, instead of having to pay a dowry, they'll get something. Oh, if only I could see her under the *chuppah* at the marriage ceremony already. And then they'll move to Halicz and I can go there every day, and the *cholent* we'll cook for *shabbes* will be so rich and juicy the whole of Halicz will go green with envy." The Yiddish words were so familiar to the *shabbes goy* that her native Ruthenian had gradually come to resemble her smock, whose blue linen had numerous patches of different materials.

Finally she was there. She flung open the kitchen door and breathlessly stammered, "*Mazeltov*. What good news! And if God wills, she'll be a widow in three months time!"

Chane got the shock of her life and shot a worried glance out into the yard, where Miriam was washing the cutlery for the sabbath. Fortunately she had not heard.

"Shhh," she said in a low voice, going over to Kasia. "Not a word more, understood?"

Bewildered, Kasia looked at her mistress and out into the yard. But then light dawned in her dull features. "She doesn't know yet?" she asked in a whisper. "But why not?"

"Because we don't know ourselves," Chane replied curtly. "Because the people in Halicz talk nonsense."

Kasia slumped onto a chair, devastated. "And I was so pleased," she wailed. So it was goodbye to her dreams of the good life, the *cholent* would be as plain as ever and would continue to be eaten here in Vinkovce; it was even goodbye to the juicy titbit of gossip that could have been chewed over for hours. And that was the worst thing about it, at least just for the moment. But why should she not talk about it? She shot to her feet. "Then at least someone should tell her what people are saying," she cried.

"Not one word!" Chane commanded, pushing her back down onto the chair.

"But why ever not?" Kasia wailed again. "People are saying the old man's crazy about her, that's why he's marrying his son off as quickly as possible, the wedding's in a fortnight's time. She must be pleased to hear that, even if it's not true... . But is it really not true?" she suddenly asked. "I know the kind of lies people tell," she went on sanctimoniously, and, indeed, Kasia did know that very well, "but to invent everything? And why was that redhead Meyerl here just now? I passed him on the way."

Chane paused for thought. To tell a gossip like Kasia the truth was impossible; she must be made to think the rumour was false. But how to stop her mentioning it at all?

Finally she thought she had found the right approach. "Listen, Kasia," she said, "it really is all a lie and it wasn't us Meyerl was visiting. It was another innkeeper who started the rumour because he wants to take over our lease. You know Paterski has threatened to throw us out, but we're negotiating with him. This man's spread the rumour so that Paterski will hear of our rich son-in-law and set conditions we can't accept. And Miriam mustn't know about this. She's still a child and shouldn't concern herself with things like that... . So if you go talking about it, you'll deprive us of our livelihood."

"Heaven forbid," exclaimed Kasia, crossing herself. "I'll be as silent as the grave of a new-born child."

And she really did intend to keep her promise. But, oh, if only keeping silent were not so difficult! Or if she only had some other spicy piece of news to relate. But during the last week nothing had happened in Halicz, except that Reb Srulze Dubs's imbecilic son had pestered a girl again and got a good thrashing for his pains—which happened regularly—and that Boguslavski the tailor had got drunk and twisted his ankle—which was not particularly exciting. Also the *Kommissyja* was coming to Vinkovce on Tuesday to mark out the track for the "iron horse", but that was of no interest to Miriam and she was working beside her in the kitchen and when you're working beside someone you must be able to talk to them! So, two hours later, Miriam learnt that people in Halicz were talking about her.

"About me?" she asked, full of curiosity. "What are they saying?"

"Can't tell you. I promised your mother."

"My mother? So she knows? But what can it be?"

"Well, what is it people generally say about a girl?"

Miriam gave her an astonished look then flushed dark red and burst out into such a peal of laughter it made Kasia start and shoot a quick, guilty glance at the room where Chane was putting the candles into the *menorah* for the sabbath.

"A lover?!" she cried, when she had recovered enough to speak. "But I'm a Jewish girl.... Or that I'm to be married? But I'm too young for that. Hahaha."

This time Chane left off her work and came into the kitchen. "What are you laughing at like that?" she asked suspiciously.

"Nothing," Kasia replied apprehensively, trying to wave away Chane's suspicions with her long arms. "Just a silly joke."

But Miriam told Chane what it was.

"I didn't say that..." the maid stammered. "Stick to the truth, Miriam. I just said people were talking...it's not my fault if she guessed…. And what harm is there even if she does know? She won't let on to Paterski…. And you say it's all lies anyway…"

Chane was seething with rage, but she kept herself under control. Common sense told her to treat the matter as lightly as possible. "Tittle-tattle," she said. "People are saying there's a rich man wants to marry you."

"To marry me?!" Miriam laughed. "A rich man?!" And she laughed and laughed till her auburn plaits were threatening to come undone.

"Yes, a load of nonsense," said her mother. "It just goes to show how nasty people can be." And she gave Miriam her explanation of who had started the rumour and why.

Then she turned to Kasia. "And now I suppose you'll go and tell all the villagers?" she asked in contemptuous tones. "So that Paterski's sure to hear of it in no time at all?"

Kasia gulped. "I'll keep silent," she assured Chane, "silent as the grave of…" She faltered, unsure what to say, since the newborn child had proved such a gossip. "…silent as a whole graveyard!" she finally blurted out, the tears pouring down her cheeks.

While all this was going on, Miriam had become very serious. She was staring down at the table, so deep in thought she had even stopped her work.

"What is it?" Chane asked sharply.

Miriam started. "It's just that…I mean…but that can't be it…I mean, do you think Janko's heard the rumour and that's why he's stopped coming?"

Chane was at a loss what to say. But then, when she saw the unaccustomed expression of embarrassment, even emotion, on her daughter's face, she drew in her breath sharply and her heart stood still for a moment as she was struck by a thought that had never occurred to her before. She had to summon up all her reserves of strength before she could ask, "What makes you say that?"

Miriam blushed to the roots of her hair beneath her mother's scrutinizing gaze. "I don't know..." she mumbled. "Anyway, it's nonsense," she went on, her voice steadier now, "why should that... . It's just that I've no idea why he's suddenly stopped coming."

Chane had pulled herself together. "Why? If you want to know that you only have to ask me, it's no secret. You know why Paterski's angry with your father, don't you? All because of that ugly oaf! But we can't lose our livelihood just because of him, so we've started discussions with the Baron again. You know that—or weren't you around when Martin, his foreman, was here yesterday? So until the lease has been renewed it's not in our interest for Janko to be seen here. We have to keep in the Baron's good books, you do see that, don't you?"

"Yes," Miriam replied haltingly, unable to repress a sigh.

"What is there to sigh about?" Chane asked sharply and repeated the question, almost shouting when Miriam did not reply at once. The terrible thought that had struck her only a few moments ago had returned, making her lose her self-control.

"There's no need to shout at me," Miriam wailed. "I know you can't stand him, but I—I like him. The poor man has no one else he can talk to in the village. I'm sure it'll be very hard on him, not being able to come and see us... . I just feel sorry for him..."

Chane breathed a sigh of relief. Miriam had spoken in the childish whine she always used in response to an undeserved scolding. And the way she was sitting there, the corners of her mouth turned down and casting uncertain sidelong glances at her mother, she looked just like a child.... No, thank God, the dreadful suspicion, the very thought of which had set Chane trembling with apprehension, had no place in that innocent heart, no place at all.

"And you wouldn't feel sorry for us if Paterski threw us out?" she countered. "Anyway, as soon as the lease has been renewed, the oaf's free to come back if you want, though what my opinion of this 'friend' is, you already know."

Feeling that was a good point on which to end the discussion, she left the kitchen.

After Chane had gone there was silence for a while. Kasia pretended she was just managing to suppress a sob and since it appeared to be costing her a great effort the kind-hearted girl eventually did her the favour of asking, "What's wrong?"

"What's wrong?" Kasia groaned, initially dry-eyed, despite some vigorous fluttering of her eyelids. "First of all you force the secret out of me, then you make me out to be a gossip. Me a gossip! Ooh…"

Now the tears really did appear in her eyes.

"If that's all it is," said Miriam with a laugh, "you must be used to that kind of accusation by now."

"But I'm not a gossip!" Kasia exclaimed. "For important things I can keep as silent as—as—" But she couldn't think of a simile commensurate with such extreme discretion, so the sentence tailed off in a fit of violent sobbing.

"But how was I to know you weren't supposed to hear about it?" she went on, recovering her composure with remarkable rapidity and in a voice that had lost its tremulousness. "Why did your mother not tell me the real reason. Now I know it."

With a triumphant smile, she held up the tin bowl, in which the white fish for the sabbath were to be served, to the light to see if there was any tiny speck of dirt left on it, at the same time giving Miriam a sidelong wink.

"What do you mean by that?" Miriam asked.

"Ah, that would be telling," Kasia said. "But the gossip knows when to keep her mouth shut, as you are about to find out. I only say things I can vouch for. If people keep things from me, is it my fault if I cause trouble? And in this case—" she started sobbing again and flickering her eyelids "—I presume the trouble's not too serious. You're a sensible girl, you'll soon get used to the idea."

Miriam was dumbfounded. "Get used to the idea? What idea?"

"Are you putting on an act, like your mother?" Kasia asked in hurt tones. "Why are you trying to keep what's going on from me? First her, then you. I can forgive her, there really was some danger, but you, why won't you trust me? You haven't got anyone else you can talk about it with. Is that all the reward I get for sticking by you?" The words came tumbling out faster and faster. "Who used to protect you, who played with you? I carried you in my arms before even you were born."

Miriam laughed out loud. "Not quite," she said, "but it makes about as much sense as everything else you've said today. What is it you're getting at?"

"What am I getting at?" said Kasia, arms akimbo. "That you've been engaged to the old Jew without being told. That your parents are keeping you in the dark because they know you like Janko and won't want to marry the old man because of that.... But you will do it," she suddenly went on in pleading tones, "even though I've let the cat out of the bag through no fault of my own…through no fault of my own—how could I have even suspected something like that? It was only when you went so red just now that I realized. You'll marry old Reb David, he'll only live for a couple of months more, then you'll be a rich young widow and can enjoy life. What's the point of bothering with Janko? He really is an ugly oaf. Please, Miriam," she went on, raising her hands beseechingly, the tears now filling her little yellow eyes without her having to strain to produce them, "take the old Jew, otherwise your mother will throw me out."

Miriam let the torrent of words flow over her without response. Her gaze became even more fixed with astonishment and her cheeks burnt an even brighter red, but she did not move. Then, suddenly, she threw her arms in the air and started to laugh—to laugh and laugh so that every dimple in her round face, her eyes, every hair on her head and every muscle in her vigorous young body joined in. It lasted for minutes, the ringing peals kept bursting from her throat, like the cooing of a dove, until the tears came rolling down her cheeks. When she could speak again, her first words were, "Oh you are silly, Kasia."

"Silly? Me? I've seen what I've seen and no one will persuade me different. You go red every time Janko's name is mentioned."

"If that were so, I'd look like a boiled lobster every day from morning to evening," she replied merrily. "No, I haven't caught what your people call 'love' for Janko. I like him and I'm used to him being around, but that's all. I've already told you, I'm too young for that kind of thing, and then a Jewish girl never 'falls in love', Kasia, never, you remember that. And all this about the old man is nonsense too. Who did you say it was?"

Kasia said his name.

Again Miriam burst into peals of laughter. "Him?! I could be his great-granddaughter." Once more she laughed until she had to sit down to catch her breath.

Kasia had turned aside, offended. "Go on then, laugh," she muttered, "no one can fool me…I'll get at the truth yet, just you see."

At the same time as his daughter was laughing so merrily, Leib was faced with another awkward encounter. As he was walking past the estate office, Janko came out. Leib wanted to go on his way with a brief greeting—the sun was going down, *shabbes* was about to begin and, anyway, what had they to say to each other?— but the Ruthene stopped him.

"Hey, Leibko," he said, "has the Baron suddenly gone mad? His man Martin came at lunchtime to ask me to go and see him, he had important business with me, he said. At first I didn't want to go, but Martin said, 'Don't throw away your good fortune,' and 'If you don't go, I'm the one who'll suffer for it,' so I went. For two whole hours Paterski kept going on at me, counting out more and more bank notes onto the table, a hundred, two hundred or five hundred crowns, what do I know? I didn't look at them, I just kept saying no. It's my orchard he's suddenly decided he must have. Crazy, no?"

"Five hundred crowns," Leib asked in astonishment. "With that you could—"

"No!" Janko said defiantly, and an alarming glint appeared in his sombre eyes. "Not one square foot of my land will belong to another, nor one hair of my girl."

Leib looked away.

"The same bed or the same grave," Janko said in a dull voice.

"I'm telling you again, it won't be my fault if you refuse to believe it." And with that, he hurried off.

The taproom was dark and empty, like all such rooms at dusk on a Friday in inns where a Jewish landlord serves and Slav peasants squander their money and strength on schnapps. Six days a week the Jew is there for the villagers, put there by God to be a butt for their wit and jokes. But from Friday evening until dusk on Saturday the Jew takes time, not for himself, the villagers would not understand, much less respect that, but for his God. And for that reason he must be left in peace. On the sabbath his *goy* can serve the customers, but at the start of his day of rest the Jew needs her to look after the lights and for other such tasks, so at that hour no villager, however boorish or thirsty he might be, would enter the inn. They believe the god to whom these hours are devoted is not the true God, but "still a god, our Lord God's father", and so they stay away. For the same reason the villagers avoid looking into the lighted room when the mother of the household blesses the candles and when the father sanctifies the meal with his prayers. They are afraid they might be compelled to laugh and that is something they would prefer not to do: you don't want to get on the wrong side of *Him*.

Usually at this time, when Leib had felt his way through the semidark taproom and opened the door to the brightly lit parlour, all the worries with which his heart was burdened lifted at the sight of his wife and child in their best clothes wishing him "Good *shabbes*". Even if he arrived before they were ready, the tallow candles in the two three-armed zinc candelabras and the white linen on the table had the same effect on him. Today it was different. The other two were waiting. Chane gave him a friendly nod while Miriam rushed affectionately over to him, but his heart remained heavy. His eyes were moist with tears as he watched his wife raise her wrinkled hands over the candles and speak the ancient words of blessing, and when his daughter came up to him, head bowed, to receive his blessing, his heart and hands trembled; as he placed his right hand on her beloved head, the tears came pouring down his cheeks. Was his blessing strong enough to protect her?

It was only when he began to pray that his spirits recovered. "God, Thou Almighty One, Thou Living, Everlasting One that reigneth over us eternally…" The longer he went on, the more strength and comfort came from the beloved, familiar words, and many a sentence, to which he had previously paid no more attention than to others, now seemed filled with meaning, as if it had been written especially for him. "Make me humble towards others, let my soul strive to keep Thy commandments. Destroy Thou the attack of those that devise evil against me and frustrate their plans. Thou that maketh peace in Thy heights, let Thy peace reign over us." He spoke the words again, and a third time, they were such a comfort to his fearful soul. Surely He would take this child into His safe keeping. And when Miriam came to him after he had finished, to call him to table, he placed his hand on her head once more, and this time it was not trembling. His blessing was not strong enough, but she was in better keeping…

8

The next morning, while the three were sitting in the parlour, praying, the inn gradually filled up, as it did every Saturday. In Vinkovce that was the most profitable day for the innkeeper after Sunday. There were two reasons for this. In the first place, many of the menfolk in the village did nothing by half, and that included throwing themselves fully into the two purposes for which Sunday was devised, namely refreshment of the soul and of the body. But is it not precisely doing things by half if you go to the church in the morning and then sit in the inn from midday until late at night, drinking as long as you can still lift the glass to your lips? At least a whole day ought to be devoted to the refreshment of the body, which is why many start on Saturday, to make it a day and a half. Some are so conscientious that they make it two and a half, since they are still lying in the inn on Monday morning. In the second place, on Saturday Kasia commanded the taproom, and the attraction of her lively tongue has already been pointed out.

Never, though, did it show itself to better effect than on that Saturday. The fact that the *Kommissyja* was coming next Tuesday to mark out the track for the "iron horse" was an important piece of news for all, though it did not give rise to much discussion. They had agreed on the attitude to adopt on Wednesday, when old Harasim, the mayor, had come back from Halicz. And it was that dignified old gentleman who gave expression to the general feeling when he declared, "If those pen pushers really do go ahead with their nonsense and insist we sell our land cheaply, then our answer will be simple. 'All right,' we'll say, 'send the track through another village. We've managed without stinking devils locked up in iron cages so far in Vinkovce and we'll stay fit and healthy without them in the future too. Or get the horse to zoom through the air over our village—one piece of magic more or less can't matter that much.' Yes, that's what I'll say in the name of our village and you'll all shout, 'The mayor's right! The mayor's right!' And then you'll see, my friends, then they'll put the crowns on the table. Oh, yes." He spoke in a calm, steady voice, since he had just started his second glass. The melancholy mood only descended on him at the twentieth.

"That's what we'll do," they all cried. Only the fat smith said, "I won't oppose that, I'll stick by the village. But I have to repeat: the price I get for the land beside my house is of no concern to me. The lower the price they give me for my land, the higher the price I'll charge them for my work. We folk in Vinkovce are more than a match for those scribblers in Halicz."

The Scheherazade of Vinkovce was a mistress of her art. It was only after this first piece of news had been thoroughly digested that she served up the second, immeasurably more spicy titbit. But being an honest woman who kept her promises, she naturally didn't divulge anything herself. She just asked questions. So she went over to the table where the two most substantial personages of the village, Harasim and Onufrij the smith, were sitting and remarked casually, but with a meaningful smile that suggested something special was coming, "Who do you think got engaged this week in Halicz? Go on, guess. Who would you least expect it of?"

She picked up the mayor's empty glass and went behind the counter to fill it. And she went very slowly and took a long time filling it, giving the two men plenty of time to exchange their conjectures. Initially there was only one point they were sure of: it must be a very old man or woman.

When Kasia had been and gone a second time, they knew it was a man, after the third time that it was a Jew, after the fourth, a rich Jew.

But that was as far as they got, since in the eyes of the villagers most of the Jews in Halicz were rich. Kasia tried to put them on the right track by telling the smith that he ought to know, but that produced no immediate result.

"Me?" Onufrij asked, scratching himself reflectively behind the ear. "Moses Erdkugel? But he's got a wife. Or old Srulko Dubs? He's married as well. Or Mortche? Or Schmulko? Or Jankel?" He owed money to most of the Jews in Halicz, and that David Münzer occasionally provided him with work, because his carters sometimes had their horses shod in his smithy, never entered his head. In fact the thought of work entered Onufrij's head only rarely. It took a long time before the villagers learnt that the rich owner of the steam sawmill was the lucky man.

It took even longer for them to find out who his chosen bride was, even though Kasia told them, "I can't tell you the name, but guess, it's someone you all know." That Miriam was meant never occurred to them. When Onufrij eventually did suggest her name and Kasia confirmed it, exclaiming, "For God's sake, you're all witnesses that I didn't tell you," some still refused to believe it. "Impossible!" some cried. "She's still a child."

"She's not exactly a child any more," laughed the smith, supporting his statement with a few coarse expressions. "And there's a man in the village..." he went on. But then he broke off, recalling the priest's warning, which put a brake on his tongue.

Others were less restrained. "What a disgrace," most cried, "to treat a child like that." Only a few defended her father. "It was the only thing stupid old Leibko could think of. And anyway, that's the way these Jews do things. Let's just hope he hasn't got so much from it he can afford to give up the lease. If he does, we can say goodbye to unwatered schnapps."

"That's the way these Jews do things." That was the opinion of Father Hilarion, too. The young priest was constantly inveighing against those who went to the inn on weekdays, but he was to be found there himself almost every Saturday. That was where he met his flock and could, if necessary, give them a good talking to. It was much more effective there than if he summoned them to come to him, or went to see them in their cottages. "My sermons on Saturday achieve much more than those on Sunday," he used to tell his fellow priests with a certain amount of justified self-satisfaction.

He was the one who defended Leibko's action most strongly, not just because he respected the little Jew, but also because of Janko. He was pleased at the news because he presumed it would put an end to the crazy, disgusting idea the devil had put into the young farmer's head. "For these damned Jews," he explained to his assembled parishioners, "marriage is just another business deal. These Jews—"

"Too true," the mayor interjected. His sole heir was his only daughter whom, after a young farmhand had made him a grandfather twice over, he had married off to a rich farmer who had been happy to take the children as part of the bargain. "The Jews—"

Father Hilarion cut him short: "—still have standards. If it was the custom among that accursed race, then every girl of theirs could go to the altar wearing the bridal wreath of innocence in her hair. How different with you, unfortunately! And you're interested in money too, the rich stick together, and so must the poor."

And he went on for a long time in the same vein, with no lack of juicy examples, to the delight of those unaffected and the dismay of those concerned. But almost more irritated than the latter was Kasia, for as long as the priest stayed in the inn, she could not talk half as much as when he was not there. So when he concluded his diatribe with a delighted, "That's one piece of news I'm glad to hear," she called out to him spitefully, "But probably nothing'll come of it, Father. Can a girl be bought and sold like a cow?"

"She will not resist," the priest replied. "That does not happen among the Jews. Their children obey their parents."

"But if she had a particular reason—?" She broke off.

"You mean because the man is too old?"

"Or another one's too young," Harasim interjected. He was against the marriage because the priest was for it, but he had nothing specific in mind when he spoke and so was astonished when Kasia, apparently horrified, cried out, "Stop! For Christ's sake, mayor, don't reveal the secret. God knows how you found out, but it wasn't me who told you, I can take my oath on that." She began to sob. "Oh, my lips are sealed, the poor child is unhappy enough as it is…" The tears had not yet appeared in her eyes, they were presumably stuck in her throat, choking her voice.

"What?!" The exclamation came from thirty pairs of lips. Some laughed, others were serious, but all were equally astounded. A Jewish girl? They couldn't believe their ears. One called out, "Nonsense! Which young Moschko's supposed to be the lucky man?"

"It's no Moschko," Kasia wailed. "Oh, if it was a Jew, it wouldn't be such a disaster. But it's…" Again she tailed off as she burst into sobs.

Fat Onufrij shot up off his seat in excitement, directing a look of triumph at the priest. But the latter also stood up and, furious, went over to Kasia. She was another who was about to learn how close together triumph and disaster are; the hour of her most successful performance was to become that of her worst defeat.

"Silence, scandalmonger," he thundered, taking her by the arm. "To defame the daughter of your employer is bad enough, would you have the effrontery to do it to an honest Christian as well?"

"Me?!" Kasia screamed. "God forgive you, Father…. All of you here, you're my witnesses…" And she pretended to be about to swoon.

But the priest was unmoved. "Come," he commanded, dragging her out of the taproom. "I will soon put an end to your prattle."

"But Father," she moaned, "they'll throw me out."

"It would serve you right," he replied and went into the parlour, still dragging the maid behind him. He found the scene that confronted him strangely moving. Little Leib was standing by one of the windows, his face turned to the east, rocking to and fro, an expression of profound contemplation on his face; his lips were murmuring the accustomed prayers and only occasionally did his eyes go to the well-thumbed book open in front of him.

Chane and her daughter were standing at the other window, both of them, like Leib, in their best clothes, they too praying, with the difference that they kept their eyes fixed on their "women's book", repeating the words of the Yiddish meditation in a low voice. "You must sanctify the sabbath through quiet and prayer, but you can best sanctify it through a good work, for all mankind should be as brother and sister to you."

The last words were interrupted by the entrance of the priest, but he had heard them. It gave him a peculiar feeling. He usually regarded them as people whom God had created in His anger, and yet he felt as if he had stepped into purer air—and not just because the windows were open. "Forgive me," he said, almost in embarrassment, "but there is something urgent I have to ask you."

Leib turned towards him in fear and astonishment, but then his eyes returned to the page and he continued his low murmur; he had reached a place in the prayer where one must never break off. Chane stepped forward, but before she could ask what had happened, Kasia threw herself, wailing, to the floor between her and the priest. Kneeling, her trembling hands raised, she groaned, "Mercy! It's not my fault if they guess everything.... And I have to talk to them, or they won't drink."

"Silence!" the priest commanded, then turned to Chane. "I was pleased to hear that your daughter is engaged to David Münzer in Halicz…"

A barely suppressed smile briefly appeared on Miriam's face and Leib gave a start. Even Chane felt a shock, but she immediately pulled herself together and said, "It's not true, Father Hilarion. If my daughter were engaged," she hastened to add, "I would surely know."

"I said it wasn't true," Kasia wailed.

"You said the girl was refusing. And why? Tell us that too."

"I said," Kasia sobbed, "that it would depend on the girl as well. Everything else they guessed."

"Lies!" thundered the priest. "I'm going to put a stop to your tricks. You will go in there now and confess to everyone you lied. And if you ever repeat the slander of your brother in Christ, then woe unto you."

He grasped the large gilt cross, which he wore, as was the custom of the Greek Catholic priests of that region, on a steel chain round his neck, and held it up to her. "You will swear that you will never name the man you have slandered—I do not want to know whom you have sinned against, but whichever Christian it is, swear."

She did. As she placed her thumb, index and middle fingers on the cross, Chane and Miriam looked away in embarrassment and Leib bent even lower over his prayer book.

"And now, come," ordered the priest.

But Kasia stayed squatting on the floor and tried to grasp him round the knees. "Have mercy, Father," she cried, and when he pushed her away, she crawled over to Chane on her knees. "Spare me that," she pleaded, "I only lied to help the inn.... If I always... always told the truth, they wouldn't come and drink. And if I have to tell them now...it'll ruin your business."

But Chane, with a black look on her face, shook her head. "This is the last *shabbes* when you will serve them," she said, and, turning to the priest, "Thank you, Father Hilarion. She must take back her words before everyone."

Kasia continued her pleading and it was a long time before she eventually stood up and followed the priest out.

While all this was going on, the villagers had passed the time with guesses as to who Miriam's Christian lover could be. Almost every bachelor in the village was named, apart from Janko. It never occurred to anyone that a girl could have fallen in love with him. Onufrij just sat there, smiling to himself. He did not want to get on the wrong side of the priest.

Kasia's confession turned out to be a less edifying spectacle than the priest had hoped. She had hardly begun her stuttering avowal than the men started laughing until the room was echoing with the roars from thirty throats, rendering her sobbing confession inaudible. The priest had to repeat it to them. "Pity," they said, "it would have made a nice story. Though of course, a Ruthene and a Jewish girl—when has that ever happened?"

Around midday the inn was almost empty. Some went home to eat, most were dragged away by their wives or farmhands. Only a few stuck it out, among them the smith. He was still sitting there smiling to himself, and when Kasia, her eyes red with tears, came over to refill his glass, he whispered to her, "You've been unfairly treated. You didn't lie."

"As God's my witness," she sobbed. "If I hadn't sworn an oath on the cross—oh, the tale I could tell."

"Really?" the smith asked, genuinely surprised. "I've long known that the oaf is after her, wants to marry her even, but I wouldn't have believed she would get involved with him. Well, who'd have thought it. It's enough to make you jealous of the clod. Only a Jewish girl, but that face, those hips—" He smacked his lips. "So you've seen them?"

She raised her hands as if to ward off temptation. "Nothing," she sobbed, "I'm saying nothing. I've sworn an oath. Oh, if only I could speak.... The things these eyes have seen! But I'm sticking to my oath. There's just one thing I'm going to do. I'm leaving. I can't stand by and watch what's going on any longer."

"Really?" said the smith. "Pity. But I'm sure you'll change your mind."

"No!" she exclaimed vehemently. "A respectable woman like me cannot put up with that kind of thing any longer. This is the last sabbath I'll be serving here."

She returned to her place behind the counter, her apron pressed to her eyes. It was really only a symbolic gesture, since her eyes were dry, but as she sat there, going over everything in her mind, the tears started to flow. It was a tangle of conflicting emotions that sought relief in tears, above all shame, and then anger, and then remorse. I'm really wicked, she thought, to say such horrible things about a nice, good-natured girl who doesn't even know what it is to be a woman yet. But she was soon comforting herself with the thought that it wasn't her fault. Her mother, she's the one to blame for everything, she told herself. First of all she tries to pull the wool over my eyes, then she gets the priest to humiliate me, and then she gives me the sack. Oh, these Jews! For years the woman's been encouraging me to lie, so that she can do a roaring trade on the sabbath, and then when, just to please her, I've got into the habit, she throws me out on the street! Oh, yes, that's the way these Jews are. The things people say about them don't go anywhere near far enough.

At exactly the same time however—it was after the meal and Leib and Chane were sitting on the bench in the yard while Miriam was curled up on a barrel, reading a story from the *Arabian Nights* in her "women's book"—the couple were wondering whether they should really get rid of their maid.

Leib, usually mildness itself, was the one who was insisting on it. "If it had been anything else she'd done," he said, "I would have forgiven her. Fifteen years she's been with us, after that long you like to stay together to the end. How often have I said that to you and stood up for her when she spoke out of turn to you or to me? She always has the things people say against us poor Jews in her mind, she's a Christian and she forgets we're her employers. But now she's slandered our child and that I can never forgive her. Anyone who can speak evil of our Miriam and ruin her reputation in the eyes of others must be very wicked, more wicked than I can imagine. And I don't want a wicked woman in my house any longer."

Chane contradicted him, of course, at first simply because he had expressed his opinion so emphatically. "There you go again," she grumbled. "At first you're too soft, and then too hard. If you hadn't taken her side all these years, it would never have come to this."

"But you yourself," he objected timidly, "even told their priest…"

"But only because that's the way things turned out," she declared. "Should I have said it's all right by me if she tells lies? I didn't really mean it seriously." That, of course, was not true, but she had changed her mind. "We must keep her on, at least until Miriam is married. Presumably she'll hold her tongue because the priest made her swear to it. If we throw her out, her desire for revenge will be stronger than her oath. Just think what a disaster it would be if Reb David were to hear about those lies."

He accepted her decision, if with a heavy heart. In the evening, after the end of *shabbes* had been celebrated in the usual way, Kasia was told she was forgiven. She pretended to cry, and after a great deal of effort did indeed have tears in her eyes, tears of self-pity. For now she was absolutely convinced she had been the victim of an injustice and it was not hypocrisy but her honest opinion when she sobbed in her Yiddish/Slav mishmash, "Don't think you're doing your *shabbes goy* a *mitzvah* by forgiving her. She's doing you a good turn by forgiving you."

In Jewish practice, the night is part of the following day, and so when twilight had thickened and three stars could be seen twinkling in the sky, the sign that a new day, a working day, had begun, Leib returned to the taproom, from which he had been absent for twenty-four hours. Not every Jewish innkeeper in the east is so strict in observing the sabbath. Leib did so not because of the written law, but because of an unwritten one he bore in his heart. Without saying so to himself explicitly, he had the feeling he would long since have collapsed under the burden of his existence if, after six days of misery in which he was subject to the villagers, the Baron and his own worries, he did not have a seventh to look forward to when he belonged to Him, to Him alone, with every thought.

Shyly he greeted his customers. He was afraid Kasia's words would have taken root after all, but it turned out better than he expected. They believed the priest, and it was only harmless teasing when they asked him, "Is it true you sold your daughter to the old man in Halicz by weight, ten crowns a pound?" He didn't even have to take it to heart when Harasim said to him— amid sobs, for he was well into his melancholy phase—"Now the same thing's happened to you. Yes, yes, my poor old Leibko, an only daughter is harder to keep an eye on that a sack of fleas." The old man didn't know what he was saying, and when another of the villagers told him off, reminding him, "None of it's true, Father Hilarion told us that," he immediately agreed, saying amiably, "Of course a sober priest will know better than a drunken mayor. Come to my arms, poor old Leibko, and forgive me."

It was long after midnight by the time the inn was empty. There were still two customers there, but they were lying under the table because no one had come to take them home. Leib left them as they were, except that he pushed a bundle of hay under their heads. Then he put out the lights and discussed with Chane how they could conceal from Kasia the fact that both of them were going to see Mendele Shadchen in the morning. Leib was hopeless at that kind of thing, but Chane knew what to do.

"It's simple," she said. "We'll tell the *goy* she has to stay until midday because I have to take the interest to Mosche in Halicz and you have business in Jezupol. You set off earlier, on the Jezupol road, then take the detour round the village and meet me at the little wood."

He agreed. But the next morning, after Chane had told Kasia and Miriam this and he, as planned, was about to set off, he hesitated.

"Shouldn't we take Miriam with us?" he whispered to his wife. "She can go with you and we'll find someone we know in Halicz to leave her with until we've sorted out the engagement. I'm afraid to leave her here by herself. Just think how easy it would be for Janko to pick up something from the other villagers. And he won't think it's a lie! I told him myself last Monday that I was going to Halicz to find a husband for her."

"Yes, very clever of you," she replied. "But we can't take her with us. In Halicz she's sure to learn the truth, and we don't want that. How long we can keep it from her is quite another matter, but first she has to be prepared before we do tell her. Anyway, the oaf won't eat her."

"But frighten her perhaps," said Leib. However, he realized they had to take the risk, and set off on his way.

Even though he took the detour round the village, he had a considerable wait at the end of the little wood before he finally saw his wife dragging herself along. He knew now how ill she was, but the sight of her faltering steps as she came along the road horrified him. He hurried up to her. "Lean on my arm," he said, with a worried squint at her pale, haggard face. Just below her eyes were two spots of red with unnaturally sharp outlines.

She pushed his arm away. "No, let's sit down," she panted.

For a long time they sat in silence underneath a tree beside the road. She stared gloomily into space and he too was visited by sad, oh, so sad thoughts. The best moment life still had to offer him was approaching: he was about to arrange the engagement of his only child. And what a disappointment the engagement was! But the feeling of self-pity only lasted for a brief moment; immediately his thoughts were with his child. Miriam had no idea her fate was being decided that day, no idea what that fate was to be. And yet she would have to bear it for many, many years, it would determine her whole life. Was that right? The question cried out for an answer.... And her poor mother. He knew this was a moment she had dreamt of for a long, long time, perhaps ever since she had first held her daughter in her arms, covering her face with kisses and tears. It was the moment that held the only happiness she could still hope for here on earth, it was the only possible compensation for all the misery life had piled on her. But could this be called happiness? Instinctively he felt for her cold, moist hand and took it between his.

But she pulled her hand away. "Stop pretending," she said harshly. "If you really felt sorry for me, you wouldn't turn a deaf ear to all my pleas."

He looked away, a tormented expression on his face.

"Leib," she said in a hoarse voice, "listen carefully, or it could be that in just a few week's time you'll be regretting this moment more than any of all the other mistakes you've made in your life. Leib, it's a dying woman who's begging you: grant me a few months of peace before I have to leave you and the child. What have we to look forward to if you refuse the money?"

"But Mosche said in his letter…" he began hesitantly.

"What reliance can we put on that?" she broke in. "He's hoping your son-in-law will pay for you. If he doesn't get his money, he'll soon change his tune. And Paterski? Did you get him the orchard? It was very important for him and I can tell you why he was suddenly so keen on it. Because the railway's going to go through that orchard."

He looked at her in dismay. "It's possible," he mumbled.

"No. Certain!" she replied. "Just as certain as that we'll be out on the street, living as beggars in a few months' time. Our daughter will take us in, you're thinking? Our son-in-law give us alms? Perhaps. But does that seem better to you? Does it hurt your pride more to make four hundred crowns the condition for agreeing to the *tnoim* now, than to accept forty as charity later?"

The look he gave her was tender but firm. "His help has saved me from having to accept charity so far," he said, "and I won't need any in the future either. I shall work."

"Am I supposed to rely on that?" she cried despairingly.

"Chane," he begged, "don't keep going on about it. I cannot. I can hear His voice telling me: Leib, you cannot do it."

"I'm afraid you'll still be hearing His voice when they're putting me in my grave," she retorted. "But that's enough of that. Let's get on."

From then on she didn't say another word during the whole two hours of the journey. Since she didn't answer his questions, he too fell silent and trudged along close beside or just behind her, to support her whenever she faltered. She put up with this, but only because she felt that otherwise she was likely to collapse.

Only when they were outside Mendele's house did Leib venture another question. "Are you agreed I should ask for the money for Miriam and demand fourteen hundred crowns for her widow's portion?"

"No," she replied sharply. "I don't want him to be able to turn us away, when we go knocking at his door, with a 'Just look at the crafty ones, they want their money twice over.' You do see that, don't you?"

He didn't answer, just meekly followed her into the *shadchen*'s office.

Mendele greeted them with the blackest look he could manage on his round face. "This is a fine mess," he said. "Meyerl has just been over to ask Reb David when it would be convenient for him to come and what does he answer? He's having second thoughts! It wouldn't have been surprising if he'd definitely withdrawn. Even a man of my talents can't do anything if the people he's got involved with out of the goodness of his heart are capable of such stupid behaviour. You can demand fourteen hundred and fifty crowns, but can you keep your mouths shut? No."

Leib started in horror, but Chane sat down on the sofa and said, with a glance at the clock, "It's half past nine. If Reb David isn't here by ten we're going home. But then our second thoughts will be our final thoughts."

Mendele turned his back on her and drummed with his fingers on the windowpane. Since Leib maintained an apprehensive silence, that was the only noise that could be heard in the room until Meyerl Spazierstock came rushing in. He appeared extremely distraught; his ginger beard seemed to be literally standing on end round his ugly, wrinkled face.

"I've just been to see him," he wailed. "He's not going on with it. 'I'm not getting involved with those blabbermouths.' Yes"—it came out as a sob—"that's what he said."

"Then we're going," said Chane to her husband, who was trembling at this devastating news, and stood up.

Mendele let them get as far as the door. Then he stopped drumming on the windowpane and turned to his assistant. "What do you think, Meyerl, shall I try myself? Or is there no point."

The little manikin shrugged his bony shoulders. "Difficult to say. Every child in Poland knows you can do lots of things no one else can. But it seems to me he really has made up his mind…"

"Then don't bother," said Chane and went out into the waiting-room, Leib following her, head bowed.

"Then who's going to pay me for everything I've done," said Mendele, grasping his hat. "I have to make one more effort, even though you don't deserve it. But first I want to know what I'll get for all this extra trouble?"

At that Chane turned round. "You still don't know me," she said with a smile. "But fortunately I know you, Reb Mosche. You arranged with Reb David, who is at least as keen on the engagement as we are, that you would tell him when we arrived. Now you're using that to squeeze out a few more crowns for yourself. But it won't work, you're still not going to get more than the ten crowns."

"What?!" he cried, now genuinely angry. "You promised me fifty yourself, ten at the start and forty out of the four hundred."

"Correct. But since we have decided to forgo the four—"

"Forgo!" Mendele flushed dark red. "No one cheats Mendele Shadchen, woman. There's some trick behind it."

"There's nothing behind it," she said calmly. "We've decided to forgo it, that's all."

"But why? Why? Leib Shenker from Vinkovce refuses three hundred and sixty crowns which are there for the asking? Three hundred and sixty?" He repeated, shouting the words.

"Yes," she replied, unperturbed.

Leib, however, felt obliged to supply an explanation, "For our child—" he began.

But she cut him short. "Leave it," she said sharply. He would probably not have got much farther anyway, so astounded was he at Mendele's behaviour. The fat *shadchen* performed one, two, three pirouettes; with his bright red face and black caftan he looked like two globes, a big dark one with a small red one on top. While he was spinning, he grabbed little Leib so that he was carried round several times, like a weak, pale moon revolving round a massive star, finally depositing him in front of Meyerl Spazierstock.

"Take a good at him," Mendele panted. "The biggest fool on God's earth. That's what a man looks like who could have money and doesn't want it."

Leib couldn't get his breath back. "I—I—" he gasped.

But Chane stepped in. "One more word like that," she said, "and we're going."

"Go then," cried Mendele. "I can find another girl for Reb David, one that's younger and heavier and has money as well. What am I saying? One girl? Two! Ten! A hundred! As many as I want. In my book there—" he pointed to his desk "—there's a fifteen-year-old girl who already weighs fifteen stones. With two thousand crowns dowry!"

"All the better. Then Reb David won't have to wait too long. Come on, Leib."

"Come on, Leib," the fat matchmaker mocked, but in desperation. "What about my money? And what am I going to do with Reb David, who's set his mind on having your daughter, and no other, to send him to his grave? He's already waiting for Meyerl to come and fetch him. The *tnoim* have been drawn up already. And the bill for the fifty crowns you're supposed to pay me."

"Then everything will have to be drawn up again," replied Chane calmly.

"Drawn up again! But why? Everything can stay like as it is. You can give the four hundred crowns to your daughter if you're fools enough not to keep them for yourselves."

"A thousand crowns as widow's portion," Chane said, "fifty crowns for the trousseau and ten crowns for you. That is what we're asking for. Make up your mind, yes or no."

Mendele clasped his head in his hands. "Meyerl," he groaned, "would you mind pinching my arm so I can tell whether I really am awake or whether it's just a crazy dream. An engagement that breaks down because one party doesn't demand enough! If anyone's ever seen the like then I, Mendele Shadchen, will become a tightrope walker. It's never happened before!…Oh, my poor weak heart can't stand it…I'll explode…. It'll drive me insane!"

But none of these dreadful things happened. The engagement contract and the bill of exchange were drawn up again and then Meyerl hurried off to fetch Reb David.

Half an hour later David Münzer drove up to the "beauro" in his britzka. Climbing down was an effort, but only because of his portliness. As he stood there before Leib and Chane, they had to admit he was more hale and hearty than most men of his age, a tall, broad-shouldered figure of imposing if corpulent proportions. His back was bent, his head bowed and his eyes looked out wearily on the world through reddened lids, but he was steady on his feet and the hand he held out with friendly condescension to his future parents-in-law did not tremble.

Long as the prelude to this strange engagement had been, the actual business was brief.

"I haven't much time," Reb David said. "Also, I know you and you know me, so what's the point of wasting our breath? Meyerl tells me you don't want the four hundred crowns. If it were anyone else, I'd be suspicious, but I know what kind of man you are, Leib. So—obviously I'm not going to force the money on you, but I promise you can have it at any time, even though it's not in the contract."

He said all this in the friendly, if superior tone he usually used when doing business with a poor man.

Chane gave a satisfied nod. "We thank you," she replied. She too spoke in measured tones. "What are your wishes regarding the wedding? Mendele thought the middle of November?"

So far Leib had stood silently behind the table on which the contract was laid out, ready for signing. He was leaning with his hands firmly on the edge of the table, his legs were trembling and his heart pounding like a hammer. His weather-beaten face, which seemed even smaller, as if squashed by the pressure of his distress, was alternately going pale and flushing bright red. "Reb David," he murmured beseechingly, "it's…"

The old man ignored him and replied to Chane's question. "There's no longer any point in putting it off," he said. "I did want to wait until my Nathan was married and I would have liked to keep the thirteen weeks of mourning for my Malke, may she rest in peace. But now that word has got round…" He smiled. "I don't know who is responsible, and it doesn't matter, but it would be childish to try and keep it a secret any longer. I think we could set the wedding for next Sunday, a week today."

"Next Sunday—that soon?" Leib asked. He wanted to shout it out loud, but the shock seemed to have paralysed his vocal chords so that all that came out was a hoarse, incomprehensible gasp.

Chane, too, was visibly taken aback. "That soon?" she said. "Miriam—" has to be prepared, she was going to say, but Reb David knew that already "—has no trousseau," she hastily added.

"But that's no reason!" cried Mendele. "In a town like Halicz you could fit out ten brides in a week, a hundred, a thousand brides. A hundred thousand brides could be fitted out in a week in Halicz. And if I know Reb David, he'll give you the fifty crowns on the spot, you only have to ask."

"That is their right," said Reb David, in rebuke, "I have to pay the fifty crowns on signing the *tnoim*. If that is all," he went on, turning to Chane, "then we can leave it at next Sunday. Later on, towards the end of October, work tends to pile up, so that I find it difficult to make myself free for a whole day."

At that Leib stepped forward. "It isn't—just—the trousseau," he stammered, in pleading tones, fixing his eyes on the old man's severe features. "You must understand—our Miriam is still—still only a child—she has to be—prepared—slowly."

Mendele gave a cynical snigger. "You can leave that to your son-in-law," he said, patting the quivering Leib on the shoulder.

Reb David could not repress a smile either. "Prepare?" he asked. "She's sixteen..."

Chane broke in. "What he means is that we haven't told her yet," she said. "But that will only take seven minutes, and we've got seven whole days. There isn't much to talk about anyway..."

"Oh but there is," Leib murmured, but she went on in a clear, firm voice, "Right then, next Sunday. We can sign the contract."

Reb David stood up ponderously, went to the table and picked up the pen, but found his future father-in-law's trembling hand placed on his.

"One thing more, Reb David," little Leib begged, pale-lipped, "just one word.... You see, my child is everything to me...and she's such a beautiful, good girl...and however hard our life of poverty was, she's always been cheerful...bright as a ray of sunshine, Reb David.... You will promise me, won't you"—his voice was breaking, but his hand grasped the old man's all the more tightly—"she'll be well looked after in your house, won't she?"

"Nonsense!" Mendele exclaimed, trying to shove Leib aside. "You don't deserve your good fortune. Don't you know who you're talking to?"

A severe look from Reb David made the matchmaker draw

back. But the look the old man now fixed on Leib Weihnachtskuchen was hardly less reproachful.

"Reb Leib," he said earnestly, "from any other man I would take your request very much amiss. However, in you I can forgive it, for—" He cleared his throat. "But I'm against unnecessary talk. Why do you ask? If you had serious reservations, you wouldn't have come. And what answer can I give? That I'll clothe and feed her well? That I'm not in the habit of beating my wife? She will be as well off with me as any young woman can be with an old husband, that I can promise you."

"Thank you," said Chane. "Forgive my husband—" she quickly corrected herself "—us. It's just that she's our only child. I'm sure you won't forget how young she is," she went on in a pleading voice, "and that all she knows is our house. You're a kind man, and you know the world, so you will be aware that it will take her time to learn what is expected of a woman in that kind of household—"

Reb David interrupted her. "Of course," he said. "My sister Rachel—she's a widow—will continue to run the household as she has done since my Malke, may she rest in peace, had to give it up; she was ill for four years, as you will know." Again he went to pick up the pen.

But again Leib's hand was placed on his. "Don't get angry," he begged, "but there is one thing I feel I must ask about your sister. People say she did not get on with your late wife...And your children—are they—I mean—will they be against my—"

The old man's face flushed with anger and he threw the pen down. But then he restrained himself.

"You are Leib, the *shlemiel*," he said in a tone that wavered between scorn and pity, "there's no point in getting worked up over every word you say. But since you have raised the matter, I will give you an answer. You will not be able to claim that I kept the truth from you. My sister Rachel and my late wife, may she rest in peace, did indeed make each other's life a misery—and, between the two of them, mine. But what was the reason? Because Malke was unable to run the household and yet did not want to hand it over, and because she was proud of her family and her dowry, and my sister Rachel would not stand any nonsense since she had come to live with us just for my sake and our family is one to be proud of too. But what about your daughter? Will she insist on running the household? Will she be proud because of her family and her dowry? As for my children, they are Jewish children, their father's wishes are their command and the woman he takes as his wife will be treated with all due respect. Of course, in their hearts they are against this marriage—in their place I would be too—if for no other reason than because everyone prefers a larger to a smaller inheritance. For my sons know—" he drew himself up proudly "—that, despite my seventy years, I am still a vigorous man whom a young and healthy wife will bear a Benjamin and, God willing, a little daughter as well. But they will accept it because I wish it, and I wish it not only because it's my right, but because it is the right thing to do. I do not need to feel ashamed of it in front of anyone." Again his head, usually bowed, was vigorously raised. "If anyone wants to criticize me for it, let them step forward."

"The very idea!" exclaimed both Chane and Mendele with one voice. Even Leib murmured something suggesting God should forbid such an undertaking. However the thought going through his head was, Oh, if only it weren't my Miriam.

The old man nodded. "What objection could there be?" he

asked. His voice was once more as calm as if he were discussing a piece of business or a passage from the Talmud. "None. Perhaps there would not be, even if I were as old as King David when they brought Abishag to him. For woman blossoms for the delight of man. But I am not like King David when they brought the Shunamite to him, I am marrying again in order to fulfil God's command, for the increase of his people is pleasing to him. A Christian or a *daytsh*, one of those assimilated Jews who imitate them, probably would not do so. He would fear the mockery of his people and keep a mistress instead, for among them that is no disgrace for an old man, while marrying again is shameful. But I, thank God, am a Jew. I have never in my whole life touched a woman other than my wedded wife, and I intend to stick by that to the end. I don't deny that I am taking your daughter because she is young and beautiful. And she won't hear much in the way of sweet nothings from me, I have no time for that, nor is it my way. But what a man like me, burdened with age and work, can do to make his wife feel happy, shall be done. And now—you should have thought of all this beforehand, Reb Leib, but I will give you one more chance. You must make your decision."

"The decision is made," Chane replied, and Leib did not object.

The engagement contract was signed. After that had been done, Reb David took out his wallet and placed a fifty-crown note on the table in front of Chane. "If that is not enough," he said, "a few crowns more will make no difference. But I should imagine she will be able to buy underwear and dresses when she's my wife as well…" And since he was in a good mood and there was no need to keep the engagement a secret any more, he sent Meyerl to fetch another carriage from the sawmill and left the one he had come in to take his future parents-in-law home. They accepted gratefully and it was with lighter hearts than on the outward journey that they set off for home.

9

In the meantime a strange scene had taken place there.

On Sunday mornings the inns are always empty until after the service. Firstly because the priests insist on it, but then also because the villagers like to sleep off the effects of their previous evening's drinking until the church bells call them to mass. Thus it happened that Kasia had two full hours with not a soul to whom she could reveal what she had discovered, namely that Leib and Chane had gone to Halicz for the betrothal of their daughter to the old man who owned the sawmill; she did not doubt for one moment that there was no other reason for which both of them would have left the inn, she knew them too well for that.

Not a soul, or at least not a Christian soul. The *shabbes goy* had revealed it to Miriam, but she had just laughed. "You're mad," she said. "If it were true, I'd know about it."

"But you Jewish girls never get asked," Kasia cried.

"Perhaps," Miriam replied, "but my parents would ask me.... Or at least my father would," she added after a pause for reflection. "He's so kind. He'd never even force me to wear a dress I didn't like, never mind marry an old man like that."

"Your father!" Kasia exclaimed scornfully. "He's the one who wears the skirt in this house and your mother the trousers. She'll have ordered him not to say anything."

"Shame on you, Kasia!" Miriam exclaimed vehemently, and her eyes flashed. "Don't let me hear you say that ever again. But there's no point in getting angry at the things you say," she went on, laughing once more, "it's all just idle gossip." And she returned to her work, a song on her lips.

Kasia went to the door. Perhaps there'd be someone she could get hold of after all. But the village street was as deserted as ever, even though the sundial on the presbytery showed that it was almost nine o'clock. Her only satisfaction was that she suddenly heard Miriam singing in the yard:

> Janko, don't come here again,
> Father's warned me—

Then she suddenly broke off. "Aha!" exclaimed Kasia in triumph and hurried round into the yard. "What was that you were singing?" she demanded.

Her jubilation was all the greater when she saw that Miriam was visibly embarrassed. "What? Oh, a song..." she replied hesitantly. "You know it."

"The song of darling Janko," Kasia said mockingly. But immediately she changed her tone. "Come on, Miriam," she pleaded, "you can confide in me. I was in love once—and he was called Janko too."

At that Miriam laughed again. "Nonsense! There's nothing to confide." But she no longer sounded entirely unselfconscious, and that did not escape Kasia.

"There isn't?" she asked. "So why did you stop singing all at once? Because you realized I could hear you?"

"No!" Miriam insisted, and in that she certainly wasn't lying.

The line about the father's warning had brought to mind the scene on the moonlit road when her father made her swear never to sing that kind of song again. But however honest her "No!" was, she could no longer remain unselfconscious and when Kasia gave her a keen look, she cast her eyes down and blushed. And suddenly, she didn't know why, the thought came to her that the reason her father might have been so strongly against the song was because it was about a Janko who wasn't allowed to come back.

"No!" Kasia mimicked. "And goes as red as a cockscomb! Hahaha." And she scurried back to her observation post in the doorway.

Now people were hastening past on their way to church, and high time, too, if they were not to miss the beginning of mass. They briefly returned Kasia's greeting, but none was prepared to stop and chat. Among the last the smith came hurrying along, with somewhat uncertain steps, still rubbing the sleep from his eyes. Kasia was delighted. Just the man, she thought, and called out to him when he was still a good way off. "Smith. A word with you."

"After mass," he said, but then stopped anyway. "What is it?" he asked, full of curiosity, seeing her hurry towards him, a look of excitement on her face. "Were they at it again last night, the two of them?"

Kasia lowered her eyes modestly, as if she were blushing. "But smith," she said, "why do you ask when you know I can't say anything. I swore an oath! And those Jews kept on begging me so long last night I promised I'd give it another go with them. So now I've got to stay here until midday because the pair of them have gone out, off to Halicz. Both of them, smith! On urgent business! 'Everything depends on it,' they said and, 'You're a good woman, Kasia,' they said, 'you know how to keep a secret,' they said, 'so you'll stay here until we've finished this important business.' Then off they went and I can't even go to mass because of those damned Jews."

"The devil they have!" he exclaimed in astonishment. "So they're selling the girl off to the old man after all, are they?"

"I've sworn an oath," Kasia hastened to reply. "But just imagine, smith, right now, at the moment when they're deciding on the wedding day, the girl still knows nothing about it."

"Nor Janko either?"

"No, definitely not."

"Pity I can't tell him the good news," said Onufrij with a laugh, "but it's the priest, I'm not going to get into trouble with the priest."

He went on to the church. His intention was to tell the others that the little Jewish girl was engaged after all, but not Janko. However, as chance would have it, he arrived at the church door at the same time as his adversary. The young farmer was late too, as usual he had used the Sunday morning to go round his fields.

And when fat Onufrij saw the dark look Janko gave him from under his slanting eyelids, he was tempted to provoke him. The priest had forbidden him to tease the ugly fellow because of his love for the Jewish girl, but did that mean he couldn't tell him about her engagement? On the contrary, Father Hilarion ought to approve of that, since it would mean the end of his sinful passion. "Morning, Janko," he said in friendly tones, "what do you say to the news?"

The yellow Mongolian face went a touch paler. "Leave me in peace," Janko said, raising his fist. "I…I…"

The smith put on a hurt look. "And there was I trying to cheer you up," he said. "I'm sure you'll be pleased to hear some good news for Leib and his daughter. They've certainly done enough for you to deserve it."

By now Janko was as pale as the whitewashed wall he was leaning against. "Leave her out of it," he mumbled. "Take my advice."

"Beast," muttered Onufrij, going into the church porch. Two steps and he would be safe. "Are you really not going to congratulate her?" he asked reproachfully. "She's engaged. In three days time she's going to marry the old Jew with the steam sawmill."

And with that he quickly disappeared into the church.

But his haste was unnecessary. For a while he would have been safe from Janko, even if he had been standing right next to him. The news had struck the young Ruthene like a blow to the head. He was stunned, his knees started to give way, his trembling hands clutched the wall for support and the blood rushed to his head, which dropped; the veins at his temples swelled and everything swam before his eyes. Then he slumped into the corner of the porch, his head back, his face as white as a sheet, his eyes closed, gasping for breath. It was a long time before he finally straightened up and looked round with staring eyes.

"Who?!" His shrill cry echoed round the porch. "Old David Münzer?!"

No one answered. The only sound was the rustling of the autumn wind in the withered leaves of the lime trees beside the church door. From inside came the murmur of prayers. He was alone.

"Old David Münzer?" he repeated in a low voice, rubbing his forehead. "It's a lie, you swine!" he cried shrilly, setting off into the church. Inside a hymn started. He drew back.

"What's the point?" he muttered. "Even if it's a young Jew, she's engaged. The swine didn't lie about that." Once more he clasped his forehead and tried to think. His brain felt as if red-hot wires were boring into it and everything was dancing before his eyes, but what was there to think about? Hadn't Leib himself told him on Monday that was why he was going to the town, and since then he had not been allowed to put a foot inside the inn. So that was the real reason...

"Ohhh!" The anguish erupted from him in a long-drawn-out, inarticulate cry, almost like the howl of some tormented beast. His fingers felt for his neck, to loosen his collar, then tore open his jerkin, his shirt, clutching so convulsively at his brown, shaggy chest that his fingernails sent the blood spurting out.

"Ohhhh!...Ohhhh!" Again and again the cry of anguish came from his pale, half-open lips. It was a sound that made the blood run cold; a dog passing the church stopped, gave a brief whimper and scampered off with its tail between its legs, looking back apprehensively.

He stayed like that for several minutes. Then his expression changed. His lips closed in a firm line, an ominous glow blazed up in his staring, glassy eyes. "I warned you, Leib" he muttered, "it's not my fault if you wouldn't believe me."

He strode with slow but steady steps down the village street towards the inn. Just once he stopped. It occurred to him that he had no weapon. But then he shook his head. "Why bother?" he muttered, "something will turn up. And perhaps..." Again the dark eyes blazed, flashing wildly this time, and he flushed a sudden, deep red. "Perhaps she'll come with me," he thought. But the comforting thought had hardly occurred to him than it was gone. "She won't," he whispered. "Then it will be a—" He did not say the terrible word, but continued on his way, slowly, but with deliberate, inexorable steps, until he reached the inn.

Kasia was still keeping watch by the gateway, and since the next person she could regale with her news was taking such a long time coming, she had made herself comfortable on the little bench beside the gate. When she saw Janko approaching, head bowed, his sombre, menacing face drained of blood, she leapt up in horror. The smith's accused him of sleeping with Miriam, she thought, and he's coming to give me a good thrashing for the calumny. For a moment she was paralysed with fear, but then she ran into the inn, through the taproom and kitchen out into the yard, where Miriam was washing the dishes, still warbling away. "Janko!" Kasia wailed, raising her hands imploringly to the girl. "Protect me, he'll kill me."

"Janko?" Miriam asked, pleasantly surprised. "Mercy!" Kasia screamed, her face twisted in fear as she threw her arms round the girl. "I didn't say anything."

Miriam disengaged herself. "Are you mad? Why should Janko harm you?"

"Because Onufrij...Jesusjosephandmary!" she shrieked. Janko was already in the yard. Again she was paralysed for a moment; only her eyes moved, flitting round the yard to find a hiding place. "Onufrij was lying," she shouted at him, stretched out her arms to ward him off, rushed over to the cellar door and disappeared in the dark opening.

Bewildered, Miriam stared at her and then at Janko. "What's

all this about?" she asked. "What did Onufrij—God of Mercy! What's happened to you!?" Her exclamation was not surprising. He was standing there staring, head and hands stretching out towards her, his face contorted, his eyes ablaze. Instinctively she stepped back. Was he drunk? But then she immediately went up to him and took his hand. "What's wrong?" she cried. "Another quarrel with Onufrij? You usually keep out of that kind of thing." He held her hand in his left and raised his right hand as if he was about to clasp her to him. The sudden onset of desire made his body tremble like an aspen leaf and his half-closed eyes glazed over. "Janko!" she admonished him, tearing her hand away from his.

At that he too drew back. "Forgive me," he stammered. Then the words came tumbling out. "Swear to me—swear to me—by God and all the saints—is it true?"

By all the saints! That helped her to recover her composure. "That wouldn't mean much," she replied, with an attempt at a smile, "but I'll tell you the truth of course, as I always do."

"Are you...are you engaged?" All he could manage was a hoarse whisper.

"So that's what it is!" she exclaimed. "No, I'm still free." She didn't really feel like joking, but instinct made her adopt that tone. "Who would want me, anyway? The old man with his sawmill? We're near enough in age, I suppose, but unfortunately nothing could be further from his mind. So that's what Kasia told Onufrij and Onufrij told you? It's all lies."

He staggered and his pent-up emotions relieved themselves in a cry of, "All lies?!"

"All lies, Janko. On my honour."

Again the exclamation, this time muffled because his throat

was choked by the onset of tears, which the next moment were streaming down his face, unstoppable, like a spring. He just stood there, leaning forward, and let them flow, laughing now and then and repeating over and over, "Lies...all lies."

"Janko?!" she cried. "What's—?" Then she stopped. With a sudden realization she understood what this was all about. Without Kasia's remarks it probably still would not have occurred to her, but now she knew. Once more a deep flush spread over her face and neck, and a quiver ran through her young, ripening body.

God of Mercy, she thought, he really has caught love for me. The poor soul! Nothing can come of it of course, he's a Christian. That, though, was the only reason that occurred to her. That the other villagers called him an ugly oaf never crossed her mind. To her he was neither ugly nor an oaf, just poor, dear Janko, whose only pleasure was chatting to her, just as she had no other friend. And seeing him standing before her, laughing and crying in the same breath, beside himself with joy that she did not belong to another, she was overcome, with the same suddenness as she had realized he loved her, by a different feeling, one she had never felt before.

Her heart was pounding and she instinctively turned away to hide her blushes. For a long time they stood there like that, neither of them saying a word, the only sound his occasional sobs or a sigh from Miriam.

By chance, Miriam had her gaze fixed on the cellar door, so she immediately noticed when Kasia's head cautiously emerged from the dark opening, her expression of fear quickly changing to a sly smile as she saw the two young people standing together, mute and prey to such intense emotion.

Miriam's plump cheeks could not go a deeper red, but in a flash the dreamy look in her eyes changed to one of anger. "Why don't you come out," she cried, "and listen to the secrets we have to tell each other?"

Hesitantly Kasia came out of her hiding place. "But I didn't say anything," she insisted. "Nor will I. Not to anyone. You can speak openly in front of me."

"That's very kind of you," said Miriam acidly, "but we have nothing to hide. Have we, Janko?" But he was still standing there, dumbstruck, looking at her with eyes shining with joy. Miriam was embarrassed. "Come on, tell us. How are things on your farm? Has the black cow calved yet?"

"The black cow?" He rubbed his forehead. "I've no idea...oh, yes, she has calved..." He gave a deep sigh. "I just can't think straight at the moment."

"So it would seem," said Miriam indignantly. "If you can't look after your farm properly any more, what can you do? You should be ashamed of yourself."

"Oh, if you only knew!" But despite his confusion, the presence of Kasia made him stop short. Even if the stupid woman wasn't there, he thought, I shouldn't say anything to her. Didn't I promise Leib I wouldn't show what I feel, neither by word nor look, if only I could see her every day? If she tells him how well I behaved today, perhaps he'll allow me to come to the inn again. So he started to tell her about the black cow and that the fields towards Halicz had already been sown with winter seed, but he had not got very far before the church bells rang again. Mass was over.

"You must go now," Miriam commanded. "You know it might cause problems for us with the Baron if people see you here."

"With the Baron?" he asked in astonishment.

"But you know that," she replied, and repeated to him what

her mother had told her. Janko was dumbfounded. "Is that the truth?" he asked. "They told me…" But naive as he was, he realized in time that he couldn't tell her the reason Leib had given him without shutting himself out of this house for ever. "Where are your parents?" he asked.

"My mother's in Halicz," she said, "and my father's in Jezupol."

"Your mother's in Halicz?"

"And my father in Jezupol," she replied with emphasis. "You know I always tell the truth. And now go. God be with you, Janko. Come on, Kasia."

Kasia trailed behind her, and when Miriam had disappeared into the house, she went up to Janko, who was still standing there as if rooted to the spot, and whispered in his ear, "She loves you. She's crazy about you. By all the saints in heaven, that's the truth. And I'm ready to help you."

"What?…What?" he cried, seizing her hand in such an iron grip she shrieked, at which he let go.

When, some time later, Kasia looked out into the yard again, Janko was only just leaving, staggering as he went.

"That opened the oaf's eyes," she muttered to herself with satisfaction. "And it might not even have been a lie."

10

It was midday when Leib and Chane returned, by separate routes, as they had left. Chane, knowing what the villagers would think if they saw them in Reb David's carriage, had it stop outside the village and trudged home the rest of the way, however exhausting she found it. Leib had to go round the village so that it looked as if he were coming back from Jezupol.

As she was saying goodbye to them, Kasia found it difficult to make up her mind whether to tell them that Janko had been there or not. Saying nothing promised decidedly more amusement for the future, since they would not keep such a sharp eye on Miriam. But to keep something to herself was against her nature and in fact she ended up saying considerably more than she knew. Thus it was that Chane was told that Janko had threatened to kill her daughter, if she married the old man, while Miriam had sworn she would throw herself in the Dniester rather than become David Münzer's wife.

The news came as a terrible shock to Chane, but she quickly recovered herself. "You're lying as usual," she said coldly. "Off you go now, I'm just glad I've got five days when I won't have to listen to you." But after the *shabbes goy* had left, she called her daughter out of the taproom and asked her if there was any truth in the story.

"Not much," said Miriam with an attempt at a smile. "Janko did come here and ask if I was engaged, but he didn't threaten me. And when I said it was all a lie, he calmed down and told me his black cow had calved."

The words were harmless enough, but the tone was embarrassed and Miriam's cheeks were burning. Chane had to press her hand to her heart, so violently was it pounding with alarm, and it was some time before she had composed herself sufficiently to reply. The right thing seemed to be to give the girl a good telling-off.

"So he told you his black cow had calved, did he?" she said. "And you've just about got the brains of a new-born calf! What business have you talking to him when you know that could cause problems for us with the Baron? And what business is it of his whether you're engaged or not?!"

"But if he asks…"

"You just don't answer. And did a properly brought-up Jewish girl like you really say something against Reb David, who's high above us and all the other Jews for a hundred miles around?"

"No," Miriam insisted. "I only said the rumour people had made up was a nonsense. We're just not suited, look at the difference in our ages for a start."

"That's not only stupid, it's impudent. You know nothing of the world. Who are you to decide who's suitable or not? A Jewish child leaves that to its parents and doesn't even think about it. That's what comes of talking to those villagers and singing indecent songs. Don't let me hear you saying that kind of thing ever again. Now go." Sobbing convulsively, Miriam left the room.

For a long time Chane stared into space, silently pondering. Did I perhaps speak too sharply, she wondered? But no, you can't be too strict in these matters. God of mercy, what if she really did say no?! Or if the oaf did get into a frenzy and caused some disaster? She wrung her hands in desperation. How could they eliminate the threat he posed? But now that was no longer the greatest danger, the most bitter misfortune they might suffer. It would be even worse if Miriam should…"No! No!" Chane exclaimed in her torment, "the God of Justice cannot want that. What sin have I committed that greater shame and misery should be visited on me than on any mother in Israel before or since?" But her devout faith was not so deeply rooted as to drive away her fear. A saying of her father's came back to her: "The wise thing to do is to help yourself, then God will help you." She pondered. I have to get her away from here, she thought. I must take her to my sister in Halicz, I must do it tomorrow. There at least she'll be safe from the oaf. Of course, we won't be able to keep the truth from her there, but we have to tell her now anyway. She'll cry, perhaps she'll even kick up a fuss, but there'll be people there to help me make her see reason. I can't rely on Leib, he sways this way and that like a reed in the wind. When she weeps, he weeps with her.

This decision gave her some of her self-assurance back; anyway, she had no time to waste brooding over things. The long-awaited autumn rains had started and it was pouring down in torrents. The taproom was fuller than usual, since the bad weather had driven those villagers of more refined taste, who usually preferred to go to Halicz to get drunk on a Sunday, into the inn. Chane and Leib had their hands full and Miriam too had to help out. Given this situation, it roused Chane to ire and the customers to fits of laughter when Janko's farmhand, the redhead Saverko, arrived in the early evening with a message from his master that

Leib was to come and see him at once, he had something important to discuss with him.

"Just like our Pan Paterski," Onufrij laughed. "However, we humbly ask our gracious Lord Janko of *Vygoda* if he would condescend to come here. With this miserable weather we all need a good laugh."

It was not until the next morning that Leib was told about Janko's conversation with Miriam and Chane's decision. His immediate reaction was one of horrified alarm, but he quickly drew strength from the thought in which Chane had sought comfort in vain. "He does not punish people that harshly," he said. "You're mistaken. Our child's heart is still on the right path."

Despite that, he raised no objection to Miriam going to stay in Halicz right away. "I do feel worried," he said. "Who knows what Janko wanted yesterday?" However, Chane's condition meant the journey had to be put off until the next day. The rain was still pouring down so heavily that she could not even have managed being driven to the market town, never mind walking there.

Leib was soon to learn what Janko wanted. While he was deep in discussion with Chane—Miriam was occupied in the kitchen—the young Ruthene came into the taproom. Chane stood up and ordered him to leave in no uncertain terms, but he came closer and said, in a grim, menacing voice, "You might be sorry later that you didn't give me a hearing. It won't take long." The tone he said it in made her think twice about repeating her command. "I'll be brief," he went on. "Why did you forbid me to come here, out of fear for your daughter or fear of the Pole?"

"We don't owe you an explanation," Chane replied, "but

there's no need to keep it a secret. We don't want you here for both reasons."

"I can dispose of both objections," said Janko. He was speaking more quickly and precisely than usual, clearly he had worked out what to say. "If I want, the Baron will extend your lease for as many years as you like."

"You're that influential, are you?" Chane mocked.

"No, but I can still promise it. The Baron wants my orchard, but I refused to listen. You know I swore two oaths: my land is staying mine and your daughter will be mine. Mine—alive or dead. But I would find it hard to kill her because I love her dearly, so I'm willing to break my oath about the land, if it helps you. Yesterday therefore, after I'd learnt that was one of the reasons why you don't want to see me here, I went to the Pole and said to him, 'Extend Leibko's lease for as long as he wants and you can have my orchard at the price you want.' He agreed. That's what I wanted to tell you yesterday and what I'm telling you now. But you have to make up your minds quickly, his offer only stands until midday."

"We thank you," replied Chane briefly, but Leib said, "We couldn't accept that, you'd be making a poor bargain with him. Do you know why the Pole wants to buy your orchard?"

"I don't care why he does," Janko answered. "Pity, though, because I could also allay your fear for your daughter. Now that I've learnt she isn't engaged, I've calmed down. And I'll stay that way, for since yesterday I know that any attempt you made to force her would be in vain. Since yesterday I know that she loves me too. Not in the same way as I love her, of course. In the first place no one could love another person the way I love Miriam, no man has ever loved a girl like this since the world began; and in the second place, she's still a child."

Leib had gone pale. He leant back, eyes closed, but Chane, trembling, thrust her head forward; her haggard features, wildly contorted, were a fearful sight. "And how do you know she loves you?" she asked, breathing heavily. "Has she told you so?"

"No," he replied, "but the way…" He began to stammer; it was presumably not a question he had anticipated. "The way she—she stood there—blushing and—a man can tell, anyway," he finally blurted out.

Strange. She had always looked on this man as an oaf, and his stammering attempt at an explanation sounded bumbling enough, and yet Chane did not doubt for one moment that his instinct was correct. Her breath was coming more and more heavily; Leib put his arm round her in apprehension, vehemently telling Janko to go.

But he stayed where he was defiantly. He misinterpreted the contorted expression on Chane's face, assuming she was laughing at him because his last remarks had come out as gibberish, so he cried out scornfully, "Anyway, Kasia told me as well. Now you know: Miriam's crazy about me. Kasia swore to me by all the saints in heaven, and Kasia's a Christian. A Christian, d'you hear, Jew, a Christian?"

"Kasia!" This time Chane really did laugh. But it was a ghastly laugh that suddenly turned into a wheezing rattle.

"Go on, laugh," screamed Janko in wild fury, "it won't stop Miriam becoming my wife. And if you won't let her be baptized, she'll be my whore! I might even prefer that, even the priest would have nothing against it. My whore, do you hear you goddammed Jew, my whore, if I want."

Chane tried to reply, but all that came from her lips was a stream of blood. "Go!" Leib shouted in a shrill voice. "You've killed her!"

Horrified, Janko stared at the sick woman, at the stream of blood pouring down Leib, who was holding her in his arms. Unable to tear his eyes away from the frightful scene, he staggered back towards the door. Miriam had heard her father's cry and came rushing in. One glance at her mother, bleeding to death, and the man by the door was enough to tell her what had happened. "Mother!" she cried out despairingly. She did not know how the words came to her lips, it was as if a voice were calling to her from the very centre of her being: "Mother…I will always obey you."

One last time the eyes of the dying woman opened wide. She tried to raise her hand, as if to stretch it out in a threatening gesture at the man who was still leaning against the door, his eyes fixed on her. Then her expression changed, became gentle and peaceful. With one final effort she let her hand sink down onto her child's head.

"Always stay—" it was scarcely audible, little more than a breath of air "—always stay a good Jewish child."

11

When, about an hour after this, Father Hilarion looked out of his study window into the storm, he saw his young landlord staggering home through the wind and rain, bareheaded and distraught. Alarmed, he invited him into his room and asked him what had happened, but it was a long time before he got an answer. The only thing he heard from Janko at first was: "Now all the two of us will share is the same grave." Finally he added, "I made the Jewish woman so angry it killed her. She cursed me before she died."

The priest, though young, was a good, wise man. Had he heard of the death of the most dissolute woman in the village, he would have immediately gone to offer the family comfort and help. But the Jew, however high the regard in which he held him personally, was nothing to do with him. It did occur to him that the poor man would be in need of help and he wondered how he would get the body to Halicz, but to assist him was, to his mind, not the business of a Christian. The young Ruthene, on the other hand, was a Christian and it was his duty to help him. So he comforted him, telling him the Jewish woman's curse would not harm him, adding that he did, however, have to put all thought of Miriam out of his head, though not because of the curse, but because it was a sin.

In the afternoon the mayor came to see the priest. "What are we going to do now, Father?" he moaned. "No village can do without an inn. The Jews from Halicz have been to take away the body, and Leibko and his daughter went with them. I asked him when they were coming back, but I got no answer. The girl's almost out of her mind with grief, saying it's her fault, she disobeyed her mother. Leibko had tears running down his face, too, and he was sobbing and whispering to himself in Jewish. 'I can't understand that,' I told him, 'won't you tell me when you're coming back or sending Kasia over? It's all right for today, we're not monsters, but the inn has to be open tomorrow, we need it.' But he just went on praying, as if I was talking nonsense, and crying and crying. It's a big problem, Father. The *Kommissyja* is coming tomorrow to decide on the route for the iron horse."

"But the officials don't need your inn," the priest objected, "Pan Paterski has invited them."

"The officials don't, but we do," the mayor replied. "Remember, Father, tomorrow's the day we're going to strike it rich. Tomorrow a pile of money's going to come into the village. That big a pile!" And he held his hand high above the table to indicate the size of the pile of bank notes. "You know the way we are, Father, you'll understand that something like that calls for a drink."

It wouldn't hurt, the priest thought to himself, if they had to wait till Sunday to celebrate. But he knew he could not express such an outrageous thought without sacrificing once and for all his popularity as a man with the common touch. He felt that his duty was to stand by his parishioners in this emergency, so he advised the mayor to despatch a messenger to the head of the

Jewish community in Halicz asking for someone to be sent to stand in for Leib.

They followed his advice. That evening, despite the continuing rain, half the village was gathered outside the closed inn waiting for the messenger to return. He brought good news. "First thing tomorrow the hunchback Schimmele's going to come with Leib's keys and stay a week. That's how long Leib and his daughter have to sit in a room in torn clothes and do nothing but pray and talk Jewish."

The villagers found that very strange, and even stranger that Chane was already buried. The bizarre custom of burying the dead before sunset on the day they die was an inviolable law for all strict Jews of the east, including the community in Halicz. "And how they cried and wailed," the messenger told them, "as if Chane had been their sister. Leibko was the one who made least noise, he just wept and stared up at the heavens."

The next morning the hunchback turned up punctually, with Kasia to look after the house. "Listen," she said, "for thirty years I've been condemned to work as a maid for Jews, but it was only yesterday I found out what a hardhearted lot they are. Miriam's behaving as if she were in despair, but that's just the fear of God. I can't talk about it, but the old woman died from the shock of hearing the girl was having an affair. And then that Leibko. Do you know what he said when people tried to comfort him? I wouldn't have believed it if I hadn't heard it with my own ears. 'The Lord gave,' he said, 'and the Lord has taken away; blessed be the name of the Lord.' As if he had lost a goat."

But she found few listeners, the people had more important things to discuss. All the men of the village had gathered in the inn to wait for the appearance of the *Kommissyja* in order to bargain with them. Everyone who had a piece of land was there, apart from Janko, who was still sitting in his room, silently brooding.

"Men," said the mayor, "we've got to have our wits about us now. They're going to come and ask who'll sell their land cheaply. And I shall say, none more cheaply than the rest. A thousand crowns a square yard. Then they can do their bargaining, but we won't let ourselves be beat down by much."

"That's what we'll do," they all agreed.

Their patience was to be sorely tried. The gentlemen of the Commission turned up at the manor house at nine, where they proceeded to fortify themselves with a breakfast provided by the hospitable Paterski. And when they finally climbed back into their carriages at eleven, they didn't drive to the inn, but to the boundary between the village and Halicz.

"What can they be doing there?" the villagers asked in astonishment. "There's no point in them choosing bits of land before they know whether they're available."

"True," said others, "but perhaps they're stupid, or think we're stupid."

When, however, the midday bell sounded and the *Kommissyja* still had not appeared, some were sent out to find out what was going on.

The news they brought caused a considerable stir. The gentlemen of the *Kommissyja* were already at work. Some were looking at pieces of paper and writing, others were putting up tripods they had brought with them, measuring distances and calling out to each other, while their workmen were hammering in posts. And all of this on land that belonged to the Pole! The posts described a wide curve, going round the wood that belonged to the village. It looked as if for the moment they were going to stick to Paterski's land.

"Cheats!" they cried. "The Pole's bribed them. They ought to ask who's willing to sell his land first and at what price, then choose. They're doing it for the Emperor, it must be done in public and everyone have an equal chance."

Only Onufrij sat there impassively. "The asses haven't even asked where the smithy is," he said contemptuously. "It's a huge detour to my house from where they started via the copper beech, where they've got to now. But if that's what they want, it's not my money they'll be throwing out of the window." He advised the others to be patient.

But the villagers were worked up, not least because of all the schnapps they had drunk. The set out "to have a word with the gentlemen". Nobody cautioned against it, even the mayor went along, though he was weeping. But that was just the effect of the schnapps, not fear of where a confrontation might lead. "They're cheating us," he sobbed, "so it won't be our fault if we beat their brains out."

Given their mood, the clash with the authorities could easily have had serious consequences. That things turned out differently was no thanks to the engineers, Englishmen and Germans who did not really understand what the approaching crowd was shouting at them, but to the magistrate and head of the Halicz district administration, Jan Willczuk. He was a Ruthene himself, even though he was Polonized to the tips of his moustache, so knew his fellow-countrymen and how to deal with them. He walked up to them calmly and said, "What do you want? Just one of you is to speak."

That made them all shout out at once, but since he simply stood there, arms crossed, surveying them with a smile on his face, they automatically quietened down and finally shoved the mayor forward. "Your honour," Harasim sobbed, "it's because of the crowns—the ground, I mean. Is our ground not as good as the Pole's?"

"Better," the official replied in sincere tones, "it's arable land. But as far as possible, we take heathland that's no use for anything else. We can't demand good land for the price we can afford to pay. Have a look for yourselves and see where the route is staked out."

They looked in the direction he was pointing, then stared at each other in amazement; where the posts had been erected was indeed mostly barren ground. Just one of them, fat Onufrij, grinned slyly to himself. "Forgive me, your honour," he said, "it's nothing to do with me, but if it's poor ground you're after, we've got plenty of that too."

A few others joined in. "Of course we have," they cried, "as much poor ground as you want. Why do you only buy it from the Pole?"

The magistrate changed colour. This was the critical moment, so he tried to get out of it with a joke. "But surely you see that the iron horse can't stagger this way and that, like one of us good Ruthenes when we've had a glass too many. Its track has to be laid out nice and carefully. These gentlemen—" he pointed to the engineers "—were in the area a few months ago and that was when they drew their line on the map. Now we're here to stake out the route and make the payments. And, since it's urgent…"

That didn't work either. "Save your breath," Onufrij broke in with a mocking smile. "If it really had been done with forethought, then the gentlemen would have taken the trouble to find out where the smithy is—do you hear, your honour, where the smithy is."

"Why?" the magistrate asked.

"Who's going to repair the iron horse here in the village if not me?" Onufrij declared.

"Hahaha!" Pan Willczuk burst out laughing and all the employees of the Commission joined in. It was such loud and hearty laughter that the villagers at first stared in bewilderment, then, a little uncertainly, joined in too.

"O thou wise smith!" Willczuk exclaimed at last, wiping the tears from his eyes, "We certainly needed your advice! The iron horse can gallop for three hundred miles without stopping, without getting injured or out of breath—because it's made of iron, d'you understand, Onufrij, of iron."

Sensing how important this moment was, he burst out into another peal of laughter. And now the villagers joined in and the magistrate exploited their good mood. "People," he cried out in his sincerest voice, "a Ruthene does not deceive his fellow Ruthenes. I swear the route has been staked out the way it has so that the horse can gallop quickly and safely through your village, and for no other reason. If it goes slowly, it stinks to high heaven, and if it falls over, not a stone will be left standing on another within a radius of ten miles! But I also swear to you that land belonging to farmers will be taken up as well."

"Which ones?" they asked, more curious now than suspicious.

Willczuk put on a roguish expression. "Ah, that would be telling, wouldn't it?" he said. "Why don't you stay here and watch us, my friends?"

So the villagers did—for a while, but since there was nothing to drink out on the heath, they left, in dribs and drabs, to go back to the inn. When the gentlemen of the Commission went to the manor house for their lunch, even the obstinate remnant followed the others, so that afterwards the engineers were able continue with their work as undisturbed as they could wish. In fact when they actually needed one of the villagers, at about four o'clock in the afternoon, they had to send Willczuk's minions to fetch him. And they had a long wait, though it wasn't the villager's fault. Szymko Mroza was perfectly willing to come and take the Emperor's crowns, only his legs wouldn't carry him any more. The magistrate's officers had to haul him to the Commission, accompanied by those of the villagers who were still on their feet.

But their curiosity found meagre reward. Willczuk asked the drunken Szymko whether he was willing to give up a strip of his land for the railway. "Yes," he replied in a tipsy drawl, "but what about the money?"

"Of course," Willczuk replied, "how much?"

"A hundred crowns a square yard," said Szymko, "or ten...or a thousand..." He couldn't remember what they had decided.

"All right," Willczuk said, "you'll tell us your price in the next few days. If we can't agree, the arbitrators will have to decide." So the stakes were set out across Szymko's land, heading for Janko's orchard.

The few remaining spectators who still had reasonably clear heads viewed this with envy and resentment. They begrudged the "skinflint", the "sourpuss", the "ugly oaf" the good fortune of "doing business with the Emperor" almost more than the Pole. They laughed scornfully when they heard the magistrate give the order to fetch Janko Vygoda from the inn. "The good-for-nothing isn't there," they shouted, "he's working on his land."

Willczuk ordered him to be fetched from there. "And you can tell him," he called out after his officers, "what good fortune awaits him. Only he has to get a move on." But it was a long time before they came back. "Your honour," they said, "he really is an oaf. He says he's not coming. 'Your iron horse is nothing to do with me,' he said, 'and my orchard nothing to do with you.' When we tried to get him to change his mind, he chased us off."

The magistrate was astonished. He had not so far come across anyone who had refused the Emperor's crowns. "I command him to come," he told them. "If he's not here, we'll stake out the line without him."

This time his messengers were quickly back. "Your honour," they said, "he's a wild animal. When we gave him your order, he went deathly pale and trembled with rage. He did follow us, but only to go to his hut. He's obviously fetching his gun, so we'd better look out."

The villagers pressed forward in their curiosity. "He hasn't got a gun," they assured the Commission, "and if the oaf really does want to start something, we'd be delighted to give him a good thrashing."

His neighbours were right, Janko did not have a gun. But he did have his axe and he was rushing with it towards the gate in the fence that separated his orchard from Szymko's land, just where the engineers and their assistants were working. When they saw the deathly pale figure with the axe in his hand, they fell back. Janko was a ghastly sight. The terrible scene the previous day had ravaged his features overnight and his blazing eyes flickered to and fro in a haggard face.

Even Willczuk felt uncomfortable, but he dutifully stepped forward. "Are you Janko Vygoda?" he asked. "The railway has to go through your orchard."

"No," was Janko's brusque and menacing reply, "it will not go through it. Find another way."

"We cannot do that," Willczuk replied. "Name your price, you won't lose by it."

"I'm not selling," was the reply. Janko's face went even paler. "I swore an oath—about that and something else," he added in a mutter, "and I keep my oaths."

"Nonsense," said the magistrate, losing patience. But he pulled himself together. "Now see reason. I am here in the Emperor's name and I tell you we need your land and we are going to have it, with or without your consent."

"Yes, yes, you oaf," the villagers shouted, "obey the man or we'll give you a good hiding."

"Just you try it," Janko retorted, standing against a tree beside the gate, so that his back was covered, and raising his axe. Willczuk repressed the anger rising within him. He whispered an order to one of his officers, then told the villagers in no uncertain terms not to provoke the man.

"But you must see," he said in his mildest tones to Janko, "that I have no choice. Perhaps you don't realize what all this is about. The railway will be a boon for everyone."

And he launched into a long speech about the advantages of the railway. In the meantime his officers, following his order, had slipped round the house and crept up on Janko through the orchard in order to disarm him. "And then," said Willczuk, "if for example you want to go to Lemberg, it used to take three days; now it will be only six—"

He got no farther. Janko did not notice the men creeping up until they were right behind him. But then he suddenly swung round and one of them was rolling on the ground, covered in blood. In his fury Janko had hit him on the head with his axe. "Come on then," he screamed, "no one's getting into my orchard alive."

For a moment everyone froze, but in the next twenty men fell on him at once, villagers, the magistrate's officers, the engineers' workmen. A minute later he was lying on the ground, tied up. They all stood round him. Another, more serious crime might have taken place, but Willczuk stepped in between them. "Get back," he commanded. "The killer must be brought to justice."

12

It was three weeks later, an October night, a cold but clear, bright autumn night. For twenty days and nights the rain had fallen, fallen in such a heavy, ceaseless downpour it benumbed the senses. It was like the wrath of God, as if all the wretched little towns and villages of the plain were to be swept away from the face of the earth. The roads were impassable, the fields around Halicz and the streets of the market town a sea of mud through which both man and beast waded gloomily. The Dniester had broken its banks and the pontoon bridge linking Halicz with the steam sawmill on the opposite bank had been under water for a week; the only communication was by boat. Cold, grey water wherever one looked, it streamed down from the sky, it gushed up menacingly out of the ground. Filled with a vague sense of foreboding, the people spent the weeks in listless contemplation of the flood until finally, one Friday morning, the mist dispersed and the sun broke through again, shining on a desolate landscape but happy faces.

There were only two people in Halicz who remained, despite the sun, in the same benumbed state: Leib Weihnachtskuchen and his child. These three weeks had been like one long, starless night to them, not just the first, during which they had kept the *shiva*, the vigil for the dead, in the miserable room in the house of

Chane's sister, the shutters closed, squatting on the floor in torn clothes, staring dully, tears almost completely dried up, at the memorial candle. It has to burn for seven days and seven nights. In memory of the dead, some say; others think it is so that the soul, which has left its abode here on earth and not yet found one in heaven, can find a place to rest on earth, as it anxiously flutters round its loved ones, watching helplessly as they have to carry on with their lives in this harsh world without them.

Leib Weihnachtskuchen was a devout Jew, far removed from any such superstition. He was convinced that He, the God of Mercy, had taken the soul of the dead woman up into His heaven and that now all poor Chane's sorrows and sufferings were at an end. And yet his heart stopped whenever the flame quivered in the draught and Miriam trembled all over and beat her breast. Then he put his arm round her and held her tight. He did not ask what was going on inside the distressed child, nor did she say.

They did not talk about it even after the week of mourning was over. For Leib and his daughter it was not over, both of them felt it could never end. But as soon as the prescribed period was past, the couple who had taken them in, Chane's sister and brother-in-law, appeared and asked them what was to happen now. They too were very poor, but they had taken Leib and Miriam in because it was a sacred duty. The burden had not been too great, since the two mourners left even the meagre food that was put before them almost completely untouched, but now they needed the room and what little food they had for themselves.

"I don't know," Leib mumbled, when they asked him. "I...give me a little time to think about it."

Necessity hardens the heart. "What is there to think about?" his brother-in-law, Schmul Ledermann, asked. "You've got your business in Vinkovce. Schimmele won't want to stand in for you out there for ever. And even if he does, it's your livelihood, not his. You've got to go back."

Miriam had hardly been listening, but now she understood what was being said and started in alarm. "Not back there!" she cried in a quivering voice and closed her eyes.

"What's all this?!" exclaimed her aunt Rachel, hands on hips. "Who's going to pay for you if you stay here, that's what I want to know? The old man over there? That's all right by me, only he has to tell us."

"The old man?" Miriam asked in bewilderment, pushing the hair back from her pale face. "What old man?"

For a moment her aunt was at a loss for words. She remembered that Miriam still did not know about the engagement. She could not learn of it at this moment, not in this way! "I thought..." she stammered, "I mean...Reb Froim...he lives across the road...he was full of sympathy at the funeral, but he can't pay..."

"Later..." Leib begged.

Schmul Ledermann shrugged his shoulders. "As you wish," he said, "but don't expect anything useful to come out of all this waiting."

When the two of them were alone again, Leib took his daughter's hand in his and pushed the hair back out of her eyes with the other. He did not ask why she did not want to return to the place where the terrible scene had taken place, nor why she did not want to see Janko again. He understood without asking. He understood everything, and his tender, compassionate heart, churned up with its own sorrow, responded in sympathy. She knew that she did not need to say anything to him. She leant her head on his breast and cried her heart out once more, as she had done so often during those last few days.

While the two of them were still sitting like that, Leib heard a high, squeaky voice outside asking for him. Recognising it at once as Meyerl Spazierstock's, he gently extricated himself from Miriam's embrace and went out.

"Reb Leib," Meyerl said in condescending tones, "I've got something for you. Ten crowns, that's what I've got." He took out his wallet and held out a bank note to Leib. "Are you not fortunate?! Reb David thinks of everything. 'To be in mourning,' he said, 'is bitter, and to be in penury is bitter, but both together is too much for one man. Take him this money,' he said, 'and if he needs more, he can have it. The funeral,' he said, 'has been paid for, and if his brother-in-law Schmul wants payment for the seven days board and lodging, I'll give him that too.' Yes," Meyerl concluded patronisingly, "you are to be envied, Reb Leib."

The unhappy man stared at the ground, his lips trembling. "I thank you," he said, "but the money… . It's just that…everything's uncertain at the moment… . First I have to ask my my Miriam…"

Meyerl behaved as if he couldn't believe his ears. Perhaps that really was the case. "What?!" he exclaimed shrilly. "What's uncertain? What do you have to ask your daughter? Do you mean—" his voice seemed to give out "—to have the engagement annulled?!" he finally shouted.

Leib waved his hands at him beseechingly. "Shhhh," he begged, "or she'll hear every word. If you knew how she feels at the moment, if you could see her now…it would move the hardest heart to tears. She cannot, she must not be told just now," he went on, his voice steadier. "And as for the money, please give Reb

David my heartfelt thanks, but I hope we can manage without it. It would be the first time in my life…Schimmele's an honest man, he's looking after the inn as a good work, a *mitzvah*, I hope he's got some money for me and will be willing to stay there longer if I ask him…"

Meyerl had recovered from his surprise, but put on a show of being all the more flabbergasted. "Forgive me for saying so," he said, clasping his forehead in his hand, "but it looks to me as if your loss has taken what little sense…. Forgive me, but what is a man to think? You refuse money, you've got enough, you say. And where does this sudden wealth come from? Because Schimmele's running your inn for you and will stay longer? But you couldn't survive on what you made from the inn even before, and now it's supposed to bring in enough for two families, yours and Schimmele's? That is madness, Reb Leib, forgive me, but there's no other word…"

Poor Leib was silent, staring at the little manikin helplessly. "You may well be right," he mumbled, "I need to sort things out, but for now…for now there are just two things I do know: I cannot accept charity and I can't go back to the inn."

"Why not?" Meyerl asked with a calculating look at Leib.

"Because my Miriam is afraid of going back there," was the reply. "You must remember what a dreadful memory her mother's death is for her…"

"And that is the only reason?" the manikin asked, his squeaky voice sharp as a razor.

Leib stared at the ground and blushed. He was incapable of lying and he didn't want to tell this man the whole truth. He could not admit to anyone that another reason Miriam did not want to go back to Vinkovce was so that she would not see Janko again.

The Ruthene was partly responsible for her mother's death and yet the one person she had been familiar with from her childhood days, and she wanted to remain a good Jewish child. Oh, he understood everything....But other people?

"Why don't you reply?" Meyerl asked in even sharper tones, if that was possible. "Could it be true...God of Mercy—" he grasped Leib's arm, and this time the shocked expression on his face was not feigned "—could it really be true what Kasia...?"

"Kasia? What stories has she been telling? She's a liar."

"God grant she was lying," Meyerl replied emphatically, and the wish was honestly meant. "She says Janko is..."

"Well?" Leib cried, beside himself and grabbing the manikin by the shoulders.

"Janko—forgive me, one shouldn't say such things, and I wouldn't have brought it up, only since you refuse to say why your daughter doesn't want to go back home, and you look so embarrassed, forgive me but, well—Kasia says Janko is your daughter's lover."

"Lies!" Leib exclaimed, flushing deep red with the hurt and outrage. "A vile calumny!"

The little manikin breathed a sigh of relief. This Leib was so stupid he never lied, moreover the tone was definitely genuine. It took a load off his mind. If Kasia had spoken the truth, then the few coppers that would have come his way from Mendele's fee as matchmaker would have been lost. A *shadchen* will resort to many tricks to bring a difficult transaction to fruition or to save one that is threatened, but to fool an honest man into taking a dishonoured girl as his bride, no one among the matchmakers' fraternity would burden his conscience with something like that.

"Thank God," he muttered. Then he remembered how

unworldly and trusting Leib was. "With all due respect to your honesty," he said, "but your daughter…can you—" he broke off for a moment, "forgive me, I'm not saying she did anything, I'm just asking. This kind of case is very rare, but Mendele and I had one only two weeks ago. The daughter of a timber merchant from Sniatyn—Ruben, the tailor's son married her a few days ago and they're already starting a divorce. So, you can vouch for her?"

"Yes," Leib declared indignantly.

"You can swear to it?"

"By anything you want. My Miriam…" he burst into tears.

The door to the little room had opened; neither of them noticed.

"By your wife's grave?"

"Yes!" Leib cried.

"Thank you, Father." Miriam was there, as pale as the wall she was leaning against, but her head was held high and her eyes flashed. "Kasia was lying! Bring her to face me, ask Janko himself."

Meyerl had drawn back in embarrassment. "Forgive me," he said, "that wasn't meant for your ears. I'll shut Kasia up, don't you worry about that. And as for Janko, we wouldn't even bother to ask him if we could, but we can't. Surely you know, he's in prison."

"God of Mercy!" Leib exclaimed. "Janko? But he's a decent fellow. How could that happen?"

Miriam gave a low cry and swayed. She held onto the door handle and listened, trembling, as Meyerl recounted the scene outside Janko's orchard. The way he told it, Janko had gone berserk and seriously wounded half a dozen villagers and officers of the court. One of the victims, he assured them, had already died. "Some people say," he concluded, "that he'll never be released. Others think he'll get ten or fifteen years hard labour. But definitely not less than that."

"Fifteen years!" Leib wailed. Miriam was silent, just her breathing was audible. The twilight was thickening and it was almost dark in the vestibule, so that Meyerl could not see her expression. That was perhaps a good thing, otherwise he might have started worrying about his share of the matchmaker's fee again.

"You're still sorry for him?" he asked reproachfully, turning to Leib. "And the people he wounded, you're not sorry for them?"

"Of course I am," Leib assured him, "but I don't know them and he was our friend, wasn't he, Miriam?"

She didn't reply. Instead she went silently back into their little room.

"Your daughter has more sense than you," said Meyerl. "But there's no point in my trying to change you. At least try to be like other people as far as the main thing is concerned. And have another think whether you want those ten crowns or not. I'll ask again in the morning. Goodbye."

He left. When Leib went back into their room, where it was completely dark now that the lamp for the dead was no longer burning, and quietly called out Miriam's name, there was no answer. She must have already gone into the neighbouring room, he thought; a mattress had been put for her next to her aunt's bed there. And indeed, when he went to the door, he could hear her sobbing quietly. He did not call out to her or try to comfort her. He could understand that pain as well.

He wanted to go outside, but the storm forced him back into the house, so he sat down on the stool where he had kept watch by the lamp for the dead and gave himself up to the thoughts that came pouring into his mind. But they were not about his or his daughter's future. He did not know where the next night would find him, where he would lay his head, nor what answer he would give Meyerl when he asked him if he wanted to annul the engagement. All his thoughts were for Janko.... So this was the terrible event his dream of the axe had foretold. The blow had fallen, but on another head and, above all, on the head of the unfortunate Janko himself...Fifteen years hard labour—a wasted life! The fact that this man had threatened his child, that he had quite rightly gone in fear of him and could now breathe a sigh of relief, all that flashed through his mind, but only intermittently, like summer lightning, and then he would beat his breast and murmur, "Lord, count it not as a sin in me if I harbour that thought too." But that was only for brief moments; it was a different thought that occupied him for hours on end: if only I had been there, this misfortune could have been averted. I would have reasoned with him, explained what it was they wanted from him and that it was only for his own good. But as it was, they shouted at him until they drove him out of his mind and he went into a frenzy—just to keep his oath.

To keep his oath! That set off the other train of thought, the one he felt was a sin, and this time it refused to go away. If Janko had committed the crime in order to keep the oath he had made about his land, then surely he would also have kept the oath he had made regarding Miriam. Perhaps He, the God of Mercy, had allowed this to happen in order to prevent a worse evil. But Leib had an answer to that thought too. If He wanted to prevent evil, He did not need to resort to such means.

It was very late by the time tiredness eventually overcame him and he fell asleep on his uncomfortable seat. When he woke on the *shabbes* morning he felt so drained and worn out it was an effort to stand up. And this weariness was not only in his limbs, but in his heart too. He felt as bleak and dreary as the world outside looked. He said his morning prayers with his usual fervour, the thought of God lifted his spirits, but when he had finished his prayers and asked himself, "What now?" he felt as helpless as ever.

That was what he was like when Miriam found him. She must have cried a lot during the night, he could tell from her eyes. And her "Good morning" was muted. When, as was his custom, he softly placed his hand on the top of her head, the corners of her mouth twitched and her eyes filled with tears. But she pulled herself together, took his hand and drew him down onto the seat beside her.

"Father," she said with an attempt at a smile, "you can't work out what we should do next and nor can I. Shall we think it over together?"

"Yes, child," he answered with a sigh.

"No," she said, "you must be brave. Yesterday I said I didn't want to go back home. You know why?" She flushed deep red, but looked him steadily in the eye.

"I know..." he replied.

"But that was nonsense," she went on. "I don't find it easy today either, even more so because I know now what Kasia said about me. But we have to. That is our livelihood—at least for the immediate future," she quickly added when he once more sighed audibly. "When the time comes, God will help us. And what has to be done should be done soon. Today is *shabbes*; tomorrow we'll visit Mother's grave and then go back to our home."

"You're right," he said, trying to repress his tears. What had made him sigh, what he found so deeply moving, was not just his pity for this poor young girl, whom fate and the malice of her fellow humans had caused such bitter pain so early in her life. A memory had suddenly come to mind unbidden: Chane had been just as firm and yet kind and gentle before hardship and the struggle to survive had made her bitter.

"You're right," he repeated, not trying to hold back the tears that slowly ran down his cheeks. "Tomorrow we'll go to your mother's grave and then home."

The next morning the storm was raging worse than ever, but it did not worry them and they got ready to go out. Just as they were about to leave, however, an unexpected visitor came in: Father Hilarion.

"Leibko, my good fellow," he said in friendly tones, "I have something to ask of you." He glanced at Miriam. "It won't take long, Miriam." She went back into the little room while the two men stayed out in the vestibule.

"Well then, Leibko," said the priest, pulling his sodden coat tighter round him as there was a strong draught, "it's about Janko. You know what's happened to him?"

"I did hear," said the little Jew, pity in his voice. "He killed one man and wounded several others."

"Is that all?!" laughed the priest. "People just can't stop exaggerating. As if his misfortune wasn't bad enough as it is. He wounded just one man, one of Willczuk's officers, though he did wound him seriously. For a few days it looked as if it might be fatal, but fortunately the fellow had an iron skull. In a couple of weeks he'll be fit as a fiddle again."

"Thank God!" Leib exclaimed, genuinely pleased. "Then his sentence won't be too severe either?"

"Oh but it will," the priest replied. "Grievous bodily harm plus armed obstruction to state officials in the course of their duties. That means he'll be sent away for at least six months—if they feel lenient. There's nothing we can do about that, but what I am trying to do is to get them to release him until the trial. Otherwise the six months can easily become a year, and in the meantime his farm will go to rack and ruin."

"Certainly, but…"

"What can you do about that? A lot! I know you won't refuse me Leibko, old friend. Well, to cut a long story short, the magistrate has asked for two people from Vinkovce to stand surety for him, so as to cover himself in case Janko should commit another act of violence while awaiting trial. I was delighted when Willczuk made that condition, but—just imagine—it's impossible. I'll be one of them, of course, but none of the villagers is willing. 'That pigheaded oaf is capable of anything,' they said. And so I thought, Leibko's a decent fellow and a good friend to Janko, he'll do it."

"Me?!" Leib cried, going pale and drawing back.

"But why not?" the priest asked. "Because he made all kinds of threats if your daughter got engaged? But it's precisely because he loves your daughter so much that he won't do anything to her."

The little Jew shook his head. "Oh yes he will," he said, "because he won't let anyone else have her."

"Oh, you Jews are all so spineless!" the priest exclaimed angrily. "Is that your friendship for Janko? But I'll turn your own argument against you. He threatened you if what should happen? If your daughter got engaged! You're not going to let your daughter get married while her mother's grave's still fresh, are you?! You'll wait at least six months. And in six months' time he'll be safely locked up in prison."

Leib said nothing, just stared into space, pondering.

"What is there to think about?" Father Hilarion cried impatiently. "To earn money out of him, oh yes, Janko was good enough for that, but, as soon as he needs help, you abandon him."

Leib did not hear; the words washed against his ears like so much noise. As in every moment when a difficult decision had to be made, he was listening to the voice inside him, to see if he could hear the one in which He spoke to him. But this time he could not distinguish it clearly. Was it His voice saying, "Set poor Janko at liberty"? Or was it the one warning him, "Protect your child from the madman"?

"I don't know..." he finally murmured and asked for time to think it over. When the priest pressed him, he said firmly, "I cannot promise. First of all I must know what..." He paused. What He wants, he had been about to say, but that was no business of the priest's. "In a few days," he said, and nothing could get him to change his mind.

The priest left in a rage. "What did he want from you?" Miriam asked when Leib came back into the room and she could tell from the look on his face how much the conversation had disturbed him.

"Don't ask me," he begged. "You know I can't tell a lie, and I can't tell you the truth either."

She said no more and got ready to go out again. But fate had decided otherwise; they were never to return to their home. Hardly had she tied her headscarf than Meyerl came in and waved Leib out into the vestibule.

"Come," he said breathlessly, "Reb David wants a word with you. He's waiting!"

"With me?" Leib asked uncertainly. "What does he want?"

"He can tell you that himself," Meyerl replied impatiently. "Come. A man like Reb David doesn't like to be kept waiting."

Probably, he thought as he hurried along through the wind and rain behind Meyerl, probably he wants to cancel the engagement. Is that good news? Is that bad news? But then he realized that could not be the reason. He wouldn't tell me himself! Even if he did believe Kasia's vile calumny, no man who is a father himself would tell another father that to his face. But then I've no idea what it can be.

It was nothing surprising. It was entirely in keeping with the character of the man Reb David was.

"Reb Leib," the old man said, "I want to get things clear. Are you going to give me your daughter in marriage or are you not? For my part, I remain true to my word. You know why. Firstly, and above all, because I like your daughter. Secondly because nothing has happened in the ten days since the engagement to make me change my mind. I have never paid any attention to the things that wretched gossip said. I knew your Chane—may she rest in peace—and I know you and trust you. Blood will tell. And I've done what I could to scotch that foul rumour. I had your *shabbes goy* examined by the provost here in Halicz. It didn't take him long to get her to admit that it was all a lie, and to swear to it before several witnesses. So that has been sorted out."

"I thank you," said Leib, deeply moved.

"Don't mention it. I would have done the same for any Jewish girl. The provost will do favours for me he probably wouldn't do for others because I am in a position to oblige him from time to time. And your daughter is betrothed to me. The only question is, do you want her to remain so and be my bride? Meyerl says you have suddenly become 'uncertain' about it. Well, is it yes or no?"

Leib was silent, but only for a few moments; this time he believed he could hear His voice clearly. "Yes," he replied with a firmness that was rare in him. It was as if he had absorbed something of the nature of the man facing him. "My Chane—may she rest in peace—wanted it. I was not against it, while she was still with us, and I can't be against it now. There is just one thing that has changed. Now I must ask my Miriam whether she wants to or not."

The old man flushed with anger, but he kept himself under control. "How am I to understand that?" he asked. "While your wife was still living you thought that was not necessary, now you think it is? I'll tell you what's behind it. In your heart you are as much against it as your wife was for it. As long as she was alive, you didn't dare say no. And you still don't dare to, but what you are hoping is that your daughter will say no."

"No, that's not it," Leib replied. "As God is my witness, no. The truth is that I have always thought our daughter should be consulted, only I was never quite sure whether it was my duty to do so or not. In the meantime something has happened which tells me that it is my duty both to you and to my child. That is why I must ask her."

"And what was this something?"

"I cannot tell you that," said Leib, "but I can swear to you that it is nothing that touches my daughter's honour."

Reb David gave him a penetrating stare, which he withstood calmly. There was a long silence in the room. The old man got up and walked up and down a few times, his step less firm than usual. He was clearly struggling to come to a decision.

Finally he stopped in front of the little innkeeper. "Ask her," he said, "and come and tell me what she says. In a matter like this I would not give way to any other man, but I will to you. You are different from most men I have so far encountered. A *shlemiel*, yes, and your brain might let you down a hundred times, but never your heart. To ask a girl is unheard of, but if you believe that you must do it in this case, then I will not oppose you."

The tears came to Leib's eyes. "How can I thank you?" he stammered.

"You have yourself to thank for it," Reb David replied. "If it hadn't been for the impression you made on me at your wife's funeral, I wouldn't have given in. I knew how you felt, and I was deeply moved to see you standing there as the people expressed their condolences. You were stricken with grief, and yet I know the words came from your heart when you said, 'The Lord gave and the Lord hath taken away; blessed be the name of the Lord.' A man who can do that without hypocrisy, a man who is so devout, so truly devout, even if he were a worse businessman than you, he is not just better, he is wiser than all the rest of us. His brain may be foolish, his heart is wise. Go and do what your wise heart bids you, Reb Leib."

And with that he gently ushered him to the door.

His mind was in a whirl as he hurried home. Now I'll be sorry if she says no, he thought. I can return the compliment he made me: he can be trusted. It was only when he had almost reached his brother-in-law's cottage that it occurred to him that he had to work out how he was going to tell her. He decided to do it as gently as possible while they were on their way to Vinkovce.

Nothing came of his plan. As soon as he entered, Miriam came up to him. "Father," she said, "it's not good if we have secrets from each other. Aunt has just told me why Meyerl has been coming to see you so often and who he took you to just now. I would prefer to have heard what my future is to be from you."

"Forgive me…" he stammered. "But nothing's settled yet. I have just told Reb David that everything depends on your agreement."

"On my agreement?" she asked in amazement. "I thought you and Mother had arranged it and I have to obey."

"If you don't want to marry him, the engagement will be annulled," he replied. "Listen to me, my child, then you decide," he said and proceeded to explain to her what was to be said for it and what against. He kept nothing from her, nor did he exaggerate. He admitted how strongly in favour of the marriage Chane had been, while adding that they had both hoped for a different and better married life for their daughter.

She listened to him in silence, without asking a single question. When he had finished, she simply said, "May I think it over? Just a few hours?"

"As long as you like," he declared.

But it did not take long. In the early afternoon she came to him, a calm expression on her face, and said quietly, "I'm willing to go ahead with it."

"Don't rush it," he begged. "Have you really thought it through properly?"

"Yes," she replied. "It's best for all of us, for Mother, for you and for me."

He was particularly moved that she named her dead mother

first. "Where she is now, your mother, may she rest in peace, knows better than you or I what is truly best for you," he said. "She is in the light, she knows what is to come, we do not. Perhaps she thinks differently about this marriage now, than when she was in the dark, as we still are…"

For a long time Miriam was silent, then she said. "I can only go by what I know was her will. 'Stay a good Jewish child,' she said with her last breath. A Jewish child does what her parents want. And I've nothing against Reb David. From what you've told me about him I respect him highly."

"And quite rightly too," he said. "But there is one more question you must answer me. You're not doing it in order to provide for me?"

"No," she said calmly, "for I know you, and I know you will not accept anything from him."

"Good," he said. "Then in God's name I'll go and tell him."

He, too, sounded composed, but when he reached the door, a strange thing happened. He suddenly stopped and staggered. She hurried over and put her arms round him. "What's wrong?" she asked, concerned. But he was incapable of replying because of the sudden flood of tears. She started to cry as well, until finally she tore herself away from him.

"Go now," she said. "It must be humiliating for a man like him to be made to wait so long. And one more thing. If he wants the wedding to take place soon, then do not object."

"But what about mourning?" he protested.

"The external signs?" she replied. "Are they important? The mourning I bear in my heart for her, and the memory of her death, that will never fade, even if I live to be a hundred."

Thus it was that Leib made no objection when Reb David expressed the wish that the wedding should take place in two weeks time. "It's best like that," he said. "Should my bride go back to Vinkovce, to live among the villagers, one or two of whom surely still believe the things Kasia told them? Or should she be a burden to people like Schmul and Rachel for longer than is necessary? You can stay here too. I can sort out the arrangement between you and Schimmele. Perhaps he'll take over your lease, that would be the most sensible solution. You won't want to live in that empty house by yourself, will you? You'll find something else, either with my help or without it, it's up to you to decide."

The bridegroom naturally took charge of the organization of the wedding. "Everything will be as simple as possible," he promised, "guests kept down to a bare minimum and no music or a big meal. If I had my way, the *chuppah* would be set up in my own house, but that is contrary to the custom, so the wedding canopy will be at the rabbi's. We are determined," he went on with a smile, "to stick to what is customary. My bride was consulted, as if she were a Christian, but I'm definitely a Jew, and an old Jew at that, so I will not visit her during the two weeks, nor see her outside the house either."

And he stuck to his promise, although it would have been difficult for him to break it anyway. By the next week it was only possible to cross the river in a rowing boat, and even that was fraught with danger. Miriam heard nothing from her bridegroom; he was even sensitive enough not to send her jewellery. And the trousseau, which her Aunt Rachel purchased for her, was limited to the essential. The two weeks before the wedding were not days of sparkle and brightness. Life in the cramped cottage was as gloomy and grey as the weather outside.

When her father watched her, sitting there with a calm, earnest expression at the window of the tiny room, sewing her trousseau by the meagre light of that terrible autumn, it often occurred to him to ask whether she regretted her decision. He fought against it for a long time until eventually—it was the Thursday evening and the wedding was to be on Sunday, assuming the bridegroom could get across to the town—the question formed on his lips.

"No," she replied, calmly returning his searching look. "What has changed to make me regret it?"

The following day was that first sunny day after the weeks of gloom. Everywhere its magic produced a different, brighter mood in the people, only with these two did its power fail. If the fine weather lasted for the next two days the wedding could certainly go ahead on the Sunday, a prospect which aroused neither joy nor sorrow in father and daughter.

The sunny day was followed by a bright, clear, cold night. Leib stayed sitting on the bench outside his brother-in-law's cottage until midnight. He did not feel the cold, nor any need for sleep. It was just one more in the long series of nights when he hoped for sleep in vain. But that night he gave it even less thought than usual. In the afternoon the priest had come to see him again to try and persuade him to stand surety for Janko, this time in more moving words than before.

"The man is going to pieces in prison," Father Hilarion told him. "If you could see him you would feel sorry for him, even if you had a heart of stone, and I know you have a soft heart, Leibko. Remember how much good you've done him already and add to all that this one, last act of kindness. You need have no worries about doing it, he's a changed man, so sad and resigned. He knows—I told him—that your daughter's getting married on Sunday. He just sighed softly, but didn't say anything, never mind issue threats or work himself up into a frenzy. So you wouldn't be running any danger. Also, I'll arrange your surety so that he's not released until Monday. By that time your daughter will be mistress of a large, well guarded house, what can happen to her then?"

Once more Leib had asked for time to think about it, this time until Sunday morning. So now he was sitting there, in the stillness of the night, listening and listening for the voice within. But he could not hear what He was telling him to do.

The next morning Miriam asked him why he had stayed awake so long. He responded with a concerned question of his own. "How do you know that?"

"I imagine very few brides can sleep just before the wedding," she replied in a strained voice, then urged him to tell her what the priest wanted.

So he finally told her. She went a touch paler, then said, "I'm only a silly girl, but do you know what I'd do in your place? I'd ask Reb David if he's afraid of Janko. If he says no, then you can do the *mitzvah*."

"You're right," he said, delighted. "That's what I'll do."

On the Sunday—once more it was a fine, clear day—he had himself rowed across the river at first light, the pontoon bridge still being impassable. Reb David was astonished to hear Leib's question. He had long known of Janko's passion for Miriam, but not that he had uttered such terrible threats.

"You'd like to do it, I suppose?" he asked with a smile. "Isn't that just like you, Reb Leib, returning good for evil, comforting him in the misfortune he's brought down on himself. But whether

I can do you the favour is another matter.... I tell you what, I'll give you a letter to the magistrate asking him to tell you whether the wild beast really has become as tame as the priest claims. And of course, if that is the case he's still not to be released until Monday."

The magistrate's reply was reassuring. "Tame as a pet poodle. You can go ahead and sign, Leibko. Between ourselves, it wouldn't just be an act of charity, you'd be doing me a favour as well. I am genuinely worried he might die on me if he stays in here."

So Leib signed his name in Hebrew letters underneath the priest's. "But he won't be released until tomorrow," he asked, still worried.

"Tomorrow," the magistrate assured him.

In the afternoon Reb David and his sister were rowed across the Dniester and the marriage ceremony was performed in the rabbi's house, as had been arranged. The wedding feast lasted longer than the bridegroom wished. He drank and ate little, his bride, sitting among the women with a calm, earnest expression on her face, almost nothing, but the other guests more than made up for them. Reb David called Miriam out from the women's chamber as soon as was decently possible, but it was still fully dark as he and his bride stepped into the boat that was to take them across the wide, black river to where the welcoming lights of his house were shining brightly on the other side.

"You'll need to row carefully, Michalko," he said to the servant, who was waiting for them, hunched up on the thwart. "You know, don't you? Towards the poplars, otherwise the current will carry us too far down."

The man muttered something incomprehensible and pushed off.

"I'm sorry to have to say," Reb David joked to his young wife, "that you must sit well away from me, nearer the middle, otherwise the boat will rock too much."

She did so, but the boat rocked even more violently. Then the servant drew the oars in and stood up.

"What on earth are you doing Michalko?!" Reb David cried. "Are you drunk?"

"Miriam!" The next moment Janko Vygoda had grasped the horrified girl. "One grave…"

In a second the boat had capsized and all three fell into the cold, black waters.

The wedding feast had continued uninterrupted. It was only two hours later, when Reb David's sister returned home to find that the newly wed couple were not there, that she realized a disaster had happened, went back across the river and interrupted the merrymaking.

"Janko!" Leib groaned and collapsed unconscious.

When the magistrate drew up his report next morning, he could explain everything. On his own authority, the gaoler had released his prisoner on Sunday afternoon and Michalko, instead of waiting with the boat, had gone to the riverside inn. But that could not bring Reb David and his young wife back to life.

After the death of his wife, Leib Weihnachtskuchen had shed many tears. This time his eyes stayed dry. Silent, a fixed expression on his pale face, he sat on the stool where he had kept the vigil for Chane, staring at the flickering flame of the candle for the dead. "Keep looking, keep looking," he groaned again and again. His hands hung down slackly, just occasionally he clasped them to his heart, as if he felt an intense pain there.

Two days later his fervent wish was fulfilled when bodies were recovered from the river, first of all Reb David's—alone—then those of Miriam and Janko. In his death throes he had grasped her hand and still clutched it in his rigid grip. It was only with difficulty that they managed to separate them.

When Leib was told that his last wish on earth had been fulfilled, he nodded quietly to himself. He raised his eyes to heaven and peace spread across his features. He still found enough strength to follow her body to its grave. When the first soil fell on the coffin, the tears came streaming down his cheeks and he cried out, in a heart-rending voice, "The Lord gave and the Lord hath taken away; blessed be the name…"

Leib Weihnachtskuchen did not manage to say the last words. He clasped his hand to his heart and fell to the ground, dead.

Also from The Ascog Press

Michael Robin: *Kyselak Was Here: Scenes from a Life*, 0-9545989-1-1, £7.50

"A fictional tale of the 'might have been' life of Josef Kyselak, a real life adventurer who wrote his name all over the Austrian Empire until he was ordered to stop by the Emperor. A legend in his own lifetime, he was also one of the first lone backpackers to explore the Austrian wilderness and the high Alps. This fictional account gives an exhilarating portrayal of a youthful hero, who rises to the challenge of daring hikes, climbs and sexually free maidens."

AP in *Buzz Magazine*

Jean Marshall: *Dance to your Daddy: A Children's Minstrelsy*, 0-9545989-2-X, £9.99 (royalties go to a children's charity)

A timeless collection of children's songs, rhymes and lullabies from around the world with words, music and full-page colour illustrations